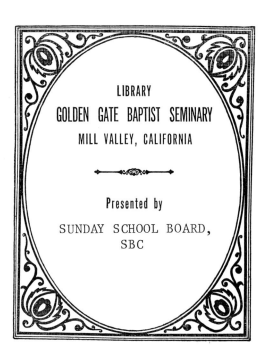

Coping with Stress in the Minister's Home

Coping with STRESS in the Minister's Home

Robert W. Bailey
and
Mary Frances Bailey

BROADMAN PRESS
NASHVILLE, TENNESSEE

© Copyright 1979 • Broadman Press.
All rights reserved.

4252-66
ISBN: 0-8054-5266-4

Scripture quotations in this publication are from the Revised Standard Version
of the Bible, copyrighted 1946, 1952, © 1971, 1973 by the National Council of
the Churches of Christ in the U.S.A., and are used by permission.

Dewey Decimal Classification: 253.2
Subject heading: MINISTERS

Library of Congress Catalog Card Number: 79-51134
Printed in the United States of America

With joy and gratitude we dedicate this book

to our children
Kevin and Courtney;
*they enrich, bless,
and strengthen our family
and
make it an exciting place
of love and happiness;*

to our parents
Mrs. Grayson Prillaman
The Reverend and Mrs. David L. Bailey, Sr.
and to the memory of
Mr. Grayson Prillaman.
*In their wisdom they have given insight,
love, and encouragement as we have sought
to follow the Divine Imperative
in our lives.*

CONTENTS

Introduction

Once as our family was traveling, we looked out the window and saw cows grazing. Strangely, they were not in the grassy field nearby, but were among the trees and underbrush adjacent to the field. They were looking for grass, but it was not able to grow under the trees. Just a few feet away was lush grass and unobstructed feeding. They were not fenced out of the grass. Either they did not know the grass was close by, or they did not know how to get to it.

Sometimes ministers and their families wander hungrily in the woods of life because they do not see or they do not know how to get to the sweet grass! Sometimes the underbrush is so dense that they get tangled and trapped. This book is designed to help ministers and their families learn how to get out of the dark woods of stress and into the beautiful pastures of God's goodness.

Webster's definition of stress is: "strain; pressure; especially, force exerted upon a body, that tends to strain or deform its shape." Therefore, stress in the minister's family that is not dealt with specifically and positively can be the factor that deforms or misshapes the idea of the family as God intended it to be.

Some may think that a book dealing with stress is a strange topic for minister's families. Because ministers preach on peace, joy, contentment, fulfillment, one might think any discussion of stress is out of place and unnecessary. The truth of the matter is that the minister's family cannot escape the fallout from all the "stress radiation" that is currently striking at the heart of home life in America. We are living in a confusing, frustrating, stress-producing society and all are touched by these aspects of life. Family life is being changed and bombarded by those who have lost sight of the truth that strength of family life is the pulse of a nation's well-being.

It is important to remember that when home life *in general* is changed, the home life of the minister is changed even more specifically. The reason for this domino effect is simply that as ministers and their families are called upon to help cope with, alleviate, or suggest cures for the problems of other families, a greater strain can occur in the minister's own family life.

What are the purposes of this book? In order to fully answer that question, let us enumerate a few things that *are not* in the purposes of this book. In the first place, the book is not designed to be an occasion for griping or complaining about the "plight of the minister's family." Secondly, our intention is not to magnify the problems of the minister's family. In the third place, the book is not supposed to offer easy, simplistic answers to a complicated problem.

Rather, our purposes are three-fold. This book is intended to be a *celebration* of the uniqueness of the minister's family. We have sought to define the particular stresses of the minister's family in light of the common stresses of all families in our society today. Guidelines for coping with ministerial stresses are offered as options for dealing with stress creatively.

Three parts comprise the book. In the first section, emphasis is given to an understanding of God's intention for the family in general. In the light of God's intention, we then note some ways that society abuses that divine design. From this backdrop we then observe and point out the potential and uniqueness that belong to the minister's family.

The second portion of the book describes eight specific stresses encountered in the minister's family. These areas of stress are: education, mobility, church, economics, time, social ties, physical and emotional, and family.

The final segment of the book draws some conclusions and offers some specific guidelines and suggestions for the means whereby the minister's family might cope redemptively and creatively with the stress it experiences.

This book offers no magic cure-all for coping with stress. Rather, it is an honest attempt to realistically define areas of stress and offer workable approaches for coping with the tempest which frequently brews in the families of ministers today.

PART 1

1 God's Intention for the Family

Several years ago a science fiction film portrayed a futuristic society in which only a select few women were given the task of childbearing. In that culture only these "second-class" women were "bothered" with birthing babies. The other women went about doing what was considered "more important" work. Compared to the Genesis account of creation, this science fiction fantasy, along with many popular notions, truly distorts God's intention for parents and for the family.

The story of the family begins with the earliest record of God and man. In the first chapter of Genesis we read that God created mankind and told them to be fruitful and multiply and have dominion over the earth. God was pleased with his creation and called it "very good!" (Gen. 1:26-31). In the parallel creation account in the second chapter of Genesis, God said that it was not good for man to be alone, so he made a helper fit for man. Woman's grandest purpose is found here—she was made by God and she was made for something—to be a helpmeet for man. And God created woman (*ishshah* in Hebrew) for she was taken out of man (*ish* in Hebrew—Gen. 2:23). "Therefore a man leaves his father and his mother and cleaves to his wife, and they become one flesh. And the man and his wife were both naked, and were not ashamed . . . . Now Adam knew Eve his wife, and she conceived and bore Cain, saying, 'I have gotten a man with the help of the Lord' " (Gen. 2:24-25; 4:1). Adam and Eve began their family with the sure knowledge of the part God played in their lives and rightfully gave him the credit.

So, from the very beginning, God had the family in mind! The Bible is filled with stories of families. Of course, biblical families had their ups and downs. In no sense were they without sin, even though their stories are in the Bible. As a matter of fact, a great deal we learn about God's intention for the family comes from inference rather than from direct example. The prophets during the last centuries before Christ had more to say about the family than did other biblical writers. One of the ancient leaders, Joshua, exemplified the family solidarity and unity before God when he declared at the edge of the Promised Land, "as for me and my house, we will serve the Lord" (Josh. 24:15). Such a declaration indicates the closeness and interdependence prevalent in this great leader's family unit. The family is in the Bible— husband and wife, father and mother, parent and child, brother and sister, grandparent and grandchild, in-laws, and throughout the extended family.

Archaeology reveals that in the earliest towns in the Mideast dating back to 5000-4000 B.C., there was a family structure. Ancient law codes, including the Mosaic Law and those codes that predate Moses, protect the rights of the family. Monogamy was the practice. Polygamy was the exception for ancient man. The Hebrew word used for family literally means "house," "box," or "an enclosure." Thus, from the Hebraic concept, we gain the understanding that the family is to be a refuge. We can grasp a beautiful picture of family as being that house or that enclosure which protects, sets boundaries, and surrounds its members. God intended husband and wife, parent and child, and including the extended family, to experience the warmth, love, security, and meaning he designed in the creation of the family.

Perhaps the strongest declaration of God's intention for the family is found in the fact of the incarnation. When God came to earth in the person of Jesus, he came as a tiny babe into a family. Does not this wonderful truth point to the significance of the family as viewed by God? He chose the family to provide the framework for the life and ministry of his Son. Luke records for us all we know of Jesus' early life. We are told that Jesus grew in body, in wisdom, and in relationship to man and God. All this growth took place in his earthly family. (See Luke 2:40,52.) Not only does this picture of Jesus' early life give us insight into God's plan for Jesus but it also sheds light upon our search for what the Bible teaches about God's intention for our families. They are to be places for growth in all areas of life—physical, emotional, mental, social, and religious.

Paul described in Ephesians 5:21 ff. the church in comparison to the family. Paul's portrayal of the church in terms of family relationships demonstrates the importance of both institutions. Both the church and the family are effective only insofar as Christ is allowed supremacy. The church is the most important institution for carrying out the work of Christ, and likewise the family is the most important institution for carrying out the work of society. In both instances, Christ is to be the head—both of the church and of the family! Neither the church nor the family discovers or fulfills its intended purpose apart from the lordship of Jesus Christ. Paul's directives to family members are plain, yet profound: Love as Christ has loved you!

When God brought the family into existence, he provided a setting for experiencing intimacy. God intended there to be intimacy between man and woman in marriage. Intimacy is a relation of creative closeness. Intimacy is a growing relation of trust and fulfillment where persons can bloom and flower. Intimacy provides a door between two people instead of a dividing wall.

After declaring that man does not need to be alone and that God made provision for the family, the Genesis writer observed that sin came in! And it was the guilt of sin that broke down the intimacy and sewed together the first fig leaves. The fundamental sin was the challenge of trying to be one's own god. Sex is not the sin. Human sexuality is the most beautiful expression of relationship between husband and wife. It is a gift that God entrusted to man and woman in the holy relationship of marriage. The sin that existed between Adam and Eve is the same sin that plagues families today. The sins of guilt, mistrust, jealousy, indifference, hatred, lack of concern cause us to sew together fig leaves and erect walls between husband and wife, between parent and child, between brother and sister, between one generation and another.

Before the fall there was a partnership in the garden. Before the entry of sin, the man and the woman worked and they enjoyed their work. They realized they were created for each other and given to each other, and in each other they found completion. Before the woman, Adam knew that in all of creation nothing completed or complemented him fully. Then when he saw Eve, he said, "at last, here is one of my own kind" (Gen. 2:23, TEV). The man and the woman saw their personhood reflected in the other. In that relationship of oneness and intimacy, they realized the completion of themselves.

Over the generations the original intent of God was one man for one woman who were married as a reflection of

authentic love. Before and during the period of the patri-
archs, marriage and family life degenerated. The pattern
of male supremacy developed. The possibility of more than
one wife replaced the one man for one woman model. The
woman became the object of a legal transaction in which
the man paid a price. The husband acquired a new name—
Ba'al, or lord and master, and the wife acquired a new
name—*Be'ulah,* or chattel property. Across the pages of
the Old Testament one can witness the attempts to return
to the original ideal of marriage. Jacob is an example of
one who was not satisfied until he was able to marry Rachel,
the woman he loved above all else. The Song of Solomon
was a treatise written on love, trying to call the Israelites
back to God's original intention for marriage. Near the end
of that flowing poetry the writer declared:

> Many waters cannot quench love,
> neither can floods drown it.
> If a man offered for love
> all the wealth of his house,
> it would be utterly scorned (Song of Sol. 8:7).

The genuine intimacy of the marriage relationship cannot
be bought and sold. It can only be given and received under
the direction and blessing of God. Remember Hosea and
the travesty of his marriage to Gomer. God disclosed
through that misuse of marriage an example of how people
forsake their commitments, both religious and marital. And
yet, out of the abiding, unending relationship of marriage
as God intended it to be, Hosea ultimately bought Gomer
from the slave block and redeemed her for his very own
(3:1-5).

There is a fundamental need for intimacy in the life of
every person. The family has the greatest potential for pro-

viding that intimacy. But for the most part, people today have allowed intimacy to decline! When we are striving to meet the expectations of others, intimacy is hard to maintain. When love is not taught and practiced in the home, the family feeds the decline of intimacy. When a young person grabs for drugs or a sexual partner to be a substitute parent he did not have, in fact, he is grasping for a sick, pseudotype of intimacy. Sex does not produce intimacy. The use of one's sexuality may be a symbolic expression of beautiful intimacy. But one's sexuality can also be arrogant, self-righteous, and hurtful both of others and of oneself. Intimacy is not easy or automatic. It requires work to develop and maintain creative closeness and a growing relationship of trust and fulfillment where each member of the family can burst into full bloom.

The whole foundation of the family God created is based on the marriage between a man and a woman. Marriage is a place for establishing nonmanipulative, growing relationships. Often two people have married but are lonely together in the same house because they have not worked at deepening intimacy. A healthy marriage is more than just doing things together. Intimacy involves being together emotionally, physically, and spiritually, while at the same time letting each other be individuals also. As Howard and Charlotte Clinebell noted in the early pages of their coauthored book, *The Intimate Marriage,* marriage is alive and intimate when husband and wife can share feelings, anxieties, hopes, dreams, and keep in good repair the bridge that joins the two of them as one.[1]

The Lebanese author, Kahlil Gibran, shares a beautiful insight into the meaning of marriage.

> Let there be spaces in your togetherness, . . .
> And stand together yet not too near together;

> For the pillars of the temple stand apart,
> And the oak tree and the cypress grow not in each other's
>   shadow.[2]

There is a need for intimacy, and there is a need for alone-
ness. We must know ourselves before we can know another,
so that a genuine I-thou, person-to-person relationship can
come alive. A poet penned some words about a meaningful
marriage which reflects on the dual nature of intimacy.

> Intimacy and autonomy
> There is within each of us
> A private place
> For thinking private thoughts
> And dreaming private dreams.
>
> But in the shared experience of marriage,
> Some people cannot stand the private partner.
>
> How fortunate for me
> That you have let me grow
> Think my private thoughts
> Dream my private dreams
> And bring a private me
> To the shared experience of marriage.[3]

Real intimacy allows continued individual growth even as
the marital relationship is made deeper and stronger.

God also intended the family to provide a secure place
to learn and develop one's self-worth. Proverbs 31:10 ff. describes a godly wife who has discovered her sense of identity
and worth in the marriage relationship. She knows the trust
of her husband. She does competent work both within the
household and with the merchants in the community. She
ministers to the poor and needy. She knows and exercises
wisdom. She takes care of her children. Her children and
husband alike praise her, and the words of her husband
stand as a glowing tribute: "Many women have done excel-

lently, but you surpass them all" (31:29). This is a beautiful example of a woman who knows that she was made by God and that she was made for something. Through the relationship of the family she is able to develop and use all of her God-given abilities.

In her book entitled *Peoplemaking,* Virginia Satir stresses the importance of each member of the family recognizing and developing his or her sense of self-worth. Parents are uniquely in the business of peoplemaking—an exalting and awesome responsibility! How we feel about ourselves colors the way we relate both to our spouse and to our children. How your children feel about being themselves affects both who they are and how they relate to others inside and outside the family.[4] Several years ago someone suggested ten important things a parent can teach a little child. At the top of the list was not how to read, not how to write, not how to tie shoes. At the top of the list of important things to teach a child were: how to gain self-confidence, how to be optimistic, and how to love being who one is.

Parents who lack personal maturity and marital intimacy will have a difficult time communicating such love to a child that will help that child have good feelings about himself. For this very reason parents need to work through their own human needs so they can be the kind of guides and helpers their children need. Every child needs guidance, security, and love. Parents who deal with their children with sensitivity will be able to love their children just as Christ loves them. This is a concept of parenting many people ignore. Parents tend either to deal with undue permissiveness with the child and thus allow the child to grow into an obnoxious, insecure, unadjusted adult, or the parents tend to use strict punishment, well-intentioned hurting, and ultimately achieve the reverse effect and develop the traits of behavior of selfishness and irresponsibility they sought to eliminate. When children are not accepted as unique, worthy individuals, they tend to reject their parents as people—including their attitudes, codes of conduct, and values which have been imposed on them.

Many Christian parents seem to forget their religious heritage when they are drawing upon their resources for childrearing. Christ teaches gentleness, trust, faith, love, kindness, and forgiveness as the foundations of healthy relationships. One has suggested that a child is a kind of "love bank" into which parents make deposits or withdrawals. A parent might make a mistake and make a withdrawal on the relationship through anger, but so long as deposits of love exceed the withdrawals, there is a balance left and the relationship remains intact.[5] Overdrafts on the account will destroy the child's feelings of self-worth and result in delinquency and prolonged behavioral and personality problems. The problems between adults and children are frequently erected by adult insensitivity to children's feelings and a failure to nurture self-worth.

"To the extent that the parent is able to manifest and maintain faith (or trust) in the child, he will enhance loving feelings and the growth of the child's conscience." [6] People are so constructed that they feel profoundly grateful to anyone who offers kindness. Parents can convey kindness through faith and trust that affirms the child's self-worth. The development of feelings of good self-worth are certainly in keeping with God's intention for the family. He valued us enough to come and dwell among us to show us how life could be lived and enjoyed more fully. He wants all of his creation to feel good about who they are!

Sensitive communication is vital to good relationships and feelings of self-worth. Virginia Satir affirms that ineffective communication patterns affect every part of life. Once in counseling a couple she heard the husband tell the wife he hated spinach though she had always served it to him. The wife exclaimed she thought he loved spinach. They had been married for thirty years, so Virginia Satir was curious enough to inquire how this spinach idea got started. The wife stated her mother had never served her father the foods he really liked—he had to eat just what was set before him. Therefore she was determined early in life to please her husband with her cooking. Through their court-ship, she never asked him what he liked—she merely ob-served what he ate and seemed to like. On one occasion before they were married they visited the husband's sister for dinner. Spinach was served. He ate two helpings. The bride-to-be translated that to mean he liked spinach, and so for thirty years she had been serving spinach two or three times a week. Sometimes he ate it and sometimes he did not. The wife thought he was not hungry or liked some other foods better when he refused to eat it. The truth of the matter was the man had eaten spinach thirty years earlier only to please his newly-married sister who was proud of her cooking! He and his sister had been reared with the teaching that it was poor manners not to eat what one was served, and in order to have good manners, one must always eat a second helping. For thirty years a man had eaten food he detested because poor, ineffective communication kept him from being truthful and kept her from asking about it.[7] With sensitivity and more direct communication, self-worth can be improved in the family in a manner and depth not possible in other places. God intended the family to be a place where self-worth is affirmed. Self-worth will de-velop both an individual and a corporate identity, not family pride in the worse sense, but in the best sense of recognizing and affirming one's heritage and identity.

In the family unit the members can teach and practice sacrificial love for each other and for the world. Many families have been weak at this point, but the family that sees itself as God's gift to one another can provide good models and concepts of love. Some common unhealthy views of love include:

"If you love me, you will never be angry with me."
"If you love me, you will always know what I want and give it to me without my asking."
"I will always see to it that you are happy and you will see to it that I am happy."
"If you love Mother and Father, you will do what we tell you." [8]

Many times we are not aware of the way in which we use our love in a dishonest or manipulative manner. God intends for the family to enable the members to grow in their ability to be honest, direct, and self-giving in their love, having no hidden agenda or strings attached to the manner or depth with which love is offered. Remember in Luke 2 how upset Mary and Joseph were when Jesus was not with them when they started home from the Temple. After they searched and finally found Jesus in the Temple about his Father's business, Jesus did not stop loving them because they misunderstood what he was to be doing. Neither did they reject Jesus or withhold their love from him.

With the help and direction of Christ, families can fulfill God's intention of developing honest, unselfish, unconditional love for one another. This kind of self-sacrificing, self-giving love was the nature of the love Paul described in 1 Corinthians 13. He wrote of an unselfish love that was not touchy and wanted the best for others. The love God offers us in Christ and desires us to share within the family and with others is not boastful, proud, destructive, or self-centered. When love for the family members among whom one lives the closest is experienced, then love for people in general beyond the family can become genuine, consistent, and Christlike. The Christian faith has always insisted that the meaning of the family is rooted in marriage which is not limited to its legal, economic, biological, social, or psychological dimensions. There is a significant additional aspect in that a Christian marriage and home is sacred and ordained of God.

In their book, *The Recovery of Family Life,* Elton and Pauline Trueblood have pinpointed three essential features of Christian marriage. One is that the marital relationship is an unconditional commitment and not simply a legal contract. A second feature is that the marriage is not a private affair but has a truly public character. The third dimension is that Christian marriage includes the willful acceptance of a bond.[9] If the idea of the family is to long endure, we must recapture these crucial elements of unconditional commitment, public sharing and example, and accepting the ties and limitations of being married to one person for life. In their chapter entitled, "The Idea of the Family," the Truebloods concluded:

The family . . . is our fairest human ideal, but it does not come without effort. Family solidarity takes hard work, much imagination and constant self-criticism on the part of all the members of the sacred circle. A successful marriage is not one in which two people, beautifully matched, find each other and get along happily ever after because of this initial matching. It is, instead, a system by means of which persons who are sinful and contentious are so caught by a dream bigger than themselves that they work throughout the years, in spite of repeated disappointment, to make the dreams come true.[10]

We are God's children. We are his family. From the beginning of time to the end of time, the family will continue to hold a vital place in God's plan for mankind. The family was the first institution in God's world, an institution that existed long before our Christian religion. It is for us to give thanks and use wisely the gift of our family. God's intention for the family includes that the family be a place, a box, an enclosure, which protects, surrounds, gives foundation, guidance, and strength to individuals within it. God intends that family members experience intimacy, learn and develop self-worth, and teach and practice sacrificial love for each other and for the world. God has a plan for the family, but oh, how we misuse it!

---

[1] Howard J. and Charlotte H. Clinebell, *The Intimate Marriage* (New York: Harper & Row, Publishers, 1970), p. 9.

[2] Kahlil Gibran, *The Prophet* (New York: Alfred A. Knopf, 1927), pp. 16-17.

[3] Lois Wyse, "A Private Place," *Love Poems for the Very Married* (Cleveland: World Publishing, 1967), p. 51.

[4] Virginia Satir, *Peoplemaking* (Palo Alto, Calif.: Science & Behavior Books, Inc., 1972), p. 3.

[5] Sidney D. Craig, *Raising Your Child, Not by Force but by Love* (Philadelphia: The Westminster Press, 1972), p. 96.

[6] *Ibid.,* p. 178.

[7] Virginia Satir, et al., *Helping Families to Change* (New York: James Aronson, Inc., 1975), pp. 208-209.

[8] *Ibid.,* pp. 142-143.

[9] Elton and Pauline Trueblood, *The Recovery of Family Life* (New York: Harper & Row, Publishers, 1953), pp. 43-48.

[10] *Ibid.,* pp. 56-57.

2

Society's Misuse of the Family

The old man's eyes were blind and his hands trembled. When he ate, he used his silverware poorly. Often he dribbled bits of food on the tablecloth. With no other place to go, he lived with his son and family. Finally the son and his wife grew weary of the old man's messiness. They took the old man gently, but firmly, to the corner of the kitchen behind the stove. There they set him on a little stool and served him his food in an earthenware bowl. One day when he trembled more than usual, his bowl fell and broke. The distraught woman scolded him, but he said nothing. As a last resort, they bought him a little wooden bowl from which he had to eat his meals.

This couple had a four-year-old son of whom they were quite proud. One evening they noticed the little boy playing intently with some pieces of wood. They asked him what he was doing. He replied that he was making a little trough for his parents to eat from when he got big. The couple looked at each other for a while without saying anything. Then they cried. Finally they went to the corner and led the little old man back to the table. Thereafter he sat in a comfortable chair and ate his food from a plate. Nobody scolded or fussed when he clattered, spilled, or broke things.

One of Grimm's fairy tales, this story has the crudity of the old, simple days. But perhaps that simplicity is necessary to make the real point. Too often parents relate to the members of the family in a pragmatic, expedient manner without taking into view the concepts and values being learned by the children. What parents do affects both who the children are today and who they will become tomorrow. Society has tended to move in one of two extremes—either the family worships the children or the family ignores the children. Either choice is unhealthy. Dr. Haim G. Ginott, noted child psychologist, has said that a newborn child has one strong emotion—fear. And his greatest fear is "of being unloved and abandoned by his parents." [1]

Doctors have observed that infants who are emotionally abused by rejection or isolation may die of starvation due to a lack of baby-mother bond! What transpires between the mother and infant during the first year is the single most crucial transaction in the family, the most significant ingredient in the shaping of the personality and future of that child! What the infant experiences during feeding and other times forms a permanent, lifelike picture of amazing consistency. Society misuses the family when it encourages the mother to miss giving this year to her infant! For the average child, the hell he fears is rejection by his parents.

Our society has taken an amazing turn during this century. Any red-blooded American would have been truly astounded and resolutely and vocally against the declaration of the nineteenth century Communist Manifesto of Marx that declared: "We replace home education by social." The basic idea of Marx was two-fold. One, children will be shifted from the family to social agencies wherein they will be taught primarily by the communistic state. And secondly, the mother will be freed of home responsibilities in order that she might be fully employed just as her husband. The breakup of the family was essential for the development of Communism. Lenin called the public nursery that freed the

mother from the burden of young children and allowed her
to hold a paying job the "germ cell of the communist
society." [2]

While the majority of Americans appear ready to fight
to "save our nation from Communism," it seems that society
is misusing the modern family in a manner not unlike what
the communistic state would! From many angles the family
is being disassembled in rapid-fire order. Journals have be-
gun to note that the "typical family" is becoming a rarity!
For years, the federal government has viewed the typical
family as comprised of four people—the husband is the breadwinner, the wife stays at home as a homemaker, and there
are two school children. Now the report has been made
that only 6.8 percent of American families fit into the classical definition of the family and 50 percent of all married
women are either working or seeking jobs, an all-time record!
Half of the mothers with children under eighteen years of
age are in the labor force. A third of the women with children
under three years of age are working. In 1950 16.7 million
women worked. In 1960 21.2 million women worked. In
1970 28.3 million women worked. In 1978 37.26 million
women worked. In many instances the women are single,
divorced, widowed, or are working to supplement their family's low income. Yet nearly half of the women work to
get "nicer things" for themselves and their families. Presently there are fewer than 16 percent of American homes
that have full-time housewife-mothers. It seems the house-
wife-mother is becoming an endangered species! [3]

Society is telling women in the last third of this century
that they are parasites, useless failures, unimaginative, or
ignorant to be content staying at home as a homemaker-
mother. However, if a woman is taking care of other children, she is thought of as some kind of heroine! Time and

again psychologists note the beginning of overt problems with children is rooted in the experience of coming home to an empty house. These problems extend all the way from slowness in learning to read, to serious depression, use of drugs, truancy, vandalism, or more serious crimes. The late Christian writer, William Barclay, wrote in his autobiography about working mothers: "I would hate a home where in the morning both husband and wife were under the pressures of getting out in time. Still more I would hate a home with no one there when I come home. And if I an adult would hate it, how much more a child? I cannot really see how anyone can run a job and a home." [4]

It is noticeable that as the political, economic, and social status of women have risen, the mystique of motherhood has declined. Between careers, available abortion, and gross selfishness, the birth rate in America has rapidly declined. After all, a baby ties the couple down! Weekend travel, professional standing, and mobility are all altered, not to mention the cost involved. Therefore a woman who is a mother—and especially a woman who seems to enjoy being a mother—is going against the current flow of pleasurable self-centeredness rippling throughout American society.

Often the father is threatened by the new mother-baby bond, to the point that a weak marital relationship may be further damaged, or a strong one weakened. The wife may use the baby to satisfy her emotional needs which the husband wants to satisfy, but may not be handling well. On the other hand, the wife may be jealous of her husband's time and resentful of having to stay at home—unable to be as free to work outside the home, to play and develop social contacts, or to come and go freely. Mothers with these feelings usually return to work quickly. And fathers with hostile feelings toward their children usually become abusers. One report estimated that more than half of all American wives are physically abused by their husbands, not to mention the emotional abuse an even larger majority of women are subjected to.[5]

Parents who had poor parents and parents who are bothered by the presence of a baby frequently demonstrate their feelings through blatant child abuse. Some sociologists fear that one out of three parents uses violent punishment—going beyond spanking—against their children. Child abuse is now recognized as a leading cause of infant mortality. Furthermore, it is estimated that one out of three female children is molested sexually by the father or another male member of the family.[6]

A family in which members are not being enabled and encouraged to move healthily through the various stages of life will add to the friction it experiences. For example, a child who experiences during the first year of his life major frustration due to lack of love, a great deal of anxiety in his home, or poor nutrition will develop a deep protest to such an unfriendly environment. That child will leave his first year totally unprepared to move into the next stages of his development. In fact, that infant will have the basic material of a parental curse in the form of a great deal of unspent rage and anger that will follow him throughout his years to come. He will have the need to go back to his first year and recover what he missed. He will have a homesickness for a time that cannot return, for a place that has vanished.

This same dynamic of turning the potential parental blessing into a curse follows all across the years of the child's life. A school-age child who is not blessed by his parents copes with life by proving his worth in terms of what he does. A child who has to shape up to his parents' requirements to receive their love must give up being a child. He is pressed to meet adult demands to the point he is unable to be a child.

A child who is not allowed to be a child when he is young will inevitably seek to be a child when he becomes older. A child who grows up with a parental curse instead of a blessing will have to unload his anxiety and depression in some manner. The psalmist captured the dilemma of many children and youth:

> Cast me not off, forsake me not,
>   O God of my salvation!
> For my father and my mother have forsaken me,
>   but the LORD will take me up (Ps. 27:9-10).

The psalmist knew where to turn in his desperation, but many people do not. They wander aimlessly through life, looking for a blessing, an affirmation.

Physically and emotionally abused children are frequently forced into the role of substitute parents, either by caring for their younger siblings or by serving as a spouse figure for the abusing parent. Reports have been filed in which a three-year-old child provided almost exclusive care for a year-and-a-half-old sibling, including carrying the child around! But when some disturbance arises between the two children, the parent usually puts down the "substitute parent" while the baby is consoled! Should there be any wonder that this child who is abused and forced to function as an adult will turn out to use and abuse others? [7]

Sometimes parents can be startled to realize the depth of the feelings of their children because they had ignored the possibility of such feelings. This was the case of the parents who received the following letter from their teenage son.

DEAR FOLKS,

. . . Remember when I was about six or seven and I used to want you to just listen to me? I remember all the nice things you gave me for Christmas and my birthday and I was really happy with the things—about a week—at the time I got the things, but the rest of the time during the year I really didn't want presents, I just wanted all the time for you to listen to me like I was somebody who felt things too, because I remember even when I was young I felt things. But you said you were busy.

I think that all the kids who are doing so many things that grown-ups are tearing out their hair worrying about are really looking for somebody that will have time to listen a few minutes and who really and truly will treat them as they would a grown-up who might be useful to them, you know—polite to them. If you folks had ever said to me: "Pardon me" when you interrupted me, I'd have dropped dead!

If anybody asks you where I am, tell them I've gone looking for somebody with time because I've got a lot of things I want to talk about.

Love to all,
Your Son

This letter was written by a teenager with a police record as a juvenile delinquent as he was moving to another city.[8]

The Grimm's tale pinpointed the attitude toward the elderly that is growing in amazing proportions based on reports now being filed about battered parents. Because they have no where else to go, the elderly often fail to report their battering to the police. Not only is there the physical abuse, referred to as "granny bashing," but also adult children abuse their elderly parents by rejecting them, abandoning them, putting them somewhere, or saying they live too long and cost too much to support. Ignoring God's directive to "honor your father and your mother" (Ex. 20:12), the care children give their parents often reflects what they were given by their parents. A declining sense of sexual morality, ease and acceptance of divorce, increasing percentage of working mothers, incessant mobility to satisfy job demands, and lack of time for family activities, are but a few of the factors that contribute to the boiling pot of family breakup in our contemporary society. The words Elton and Pauline Trueblood penned a quarter century ago are still appropriate for this generation: "Of all the disintegrating factors the chief is the loss of the sense of meaning of what a family ought to be. Our basic failure is not the failure to live up to a standard that is accepted, but rather the failure to keep the standard clear!" [9]

Many Americans have been lulled to sleep by the notion that they were providing for their family's needs if they had a fine, luxurious, comfortable house, though there might never be a genuine home established in that house! Others have felt comfortable in allowing the numerous social and civic organizations to take over functions that once were integral to the family. Not only are organizations that offer "advantages" well thought of in today's society, but also they have been given the seat of honor over and above the family.

A University of North Carolina pediatric researcher wrote that parents and the home are more important in the child's development than teachers and school.[10] Because the family is the cornerstone of a stable society, the school, the club, and the social agencies should be in business to serve the family, not take the place of the family! Society has relegated to institutions the teaching and training the family has refused to give. If there still were families old-fashioned enough for the parents to wish to play games with the children, to have family worship, to read to the children, to listen to the children, there would be little need for all these other organizations to be in the business of child-rearing and child-entertainment.

Few Americans are willing to be called Marxists, and yet, so many have adopted a great deal of the ideology that declares home education will be replaced by social! Too many parents are so engulfed in their own activities and so enamored by the "system" that they do not even seem to mind when someone else tells them they are not the best persons to handle and teach their children.

Parents who are too busy with their own desires and goals have long since abdicated their commitment to the best possible parenting. Our society has willingly embraced numerous "substitute parents," all the way from day-care and kindergarten workers to scout leaders, teachers, and coaches. In the midst of "doing their own thing" and working to climb the ladder of success that holds more material rewards, parents have allowed their precious years with their children to slip through their fingers—years that can never be recalled.

Turning to a drug, religious cult, and/or sex-oriented life-style is quite easy for a teenager who has not had his needs resolved in his own home. Such alternative life-styles promise and provide the missing ingredients of companionship, love, someone to follow, someone to talk to, group-sanctioned rationalizations for hostility and failure, and the temporary feeling that a dejected youth has somewhere to go.[11] These groups also promise, but seldom deliver, relief from depression and a lasting purpose in living. But these groups clearly speak to a need ignored by many contemporary nuclear families. Several years ago a Columbia University psychoanalyst reported on the young people involved in religious cults: "I've never seen one of these young people who didn't have some kind of serious failure in family life. They're turning desperately from the pain of the outside world to the childlike support and structures of a make-believe family." [12]

The People's Temple of Jim Jones in Guyana may remain a lasting reminder of the nature of response some people will make to anyone and anything that promises fulfillment and a better life. This is definitely not a wholesale indictment on the families of those participants in this cult. It is an attempt to focus on the growing attractiveness of cults, groups, organizations, parties, and religions that promise to provide some of the warmth, security, purpose, and direction that is absent in many contemporary homes. People who are affirmed as persons of worth during their childhood will have no room for cults as teenagers or adults. People who have been taught they are someone in the sight of God will not have to succumb to the dictatorial whims of some egotistical, distorted false god. People who have been able to spend enough time with loving parents learn to think on their own and are not forced to seek and follow an authoritarian figure who will milk, blind, manipulate, humiliate, and ultimately destroy them.

Sometimes we become so accustomed to our family that we forget they are a gift from God! Likewise, adults fail to work their way through the labyrinthine passages from one phase of adulthood to the next, thereby clogging up the volume of pressure and ignored feelings within husband and wife. We have become so bent on increasing our spending and getting that we have frequently lost sight of the value of our family and the importance of understanding and dealing with our transition points in life. Our nation has birthed a generation of people accustomed to gratifying every whim instantaneously, driven by the desire for the latest model that has immediate obsolescence built into it.

And our "thing-oriented" society has been rebelled against by the youth of the 1960's, only now to be reembraced by the youth of the 1970's. Frustration is heightened in parents by the reaction of their children. Parents are dependent on their children, not necessarily because they are close to them, but because they lean on them for some sense of continuing their youth. More and more youth are being alienated from adults who try to look, act, talk, and think like young people. Far too many families are missing the ingredient of having parents who invest love for, trust in, and commitment to the family unit.

The work week has been shortened and the average income, after adjustment for inflation, has nearly doubled in the last three decades. The result is that there is more time and money to spend on leisure activities. The sad note on the decade from 1965-1975 when there was an 11 percent increase in leisure time was that the time concentrated on family care and activities declined almost 25 percent! Now almost half our society indicates watching television is their favorite pastime.[13] The average child spends 1,100 hours a year in school and 1,500 hours watching television. The child is not coping with life but is watching others cope and is only being entertained instead of developing skills and learning to interact with others.

Meanwhile, couples are needing time together to listen to one another and build a growing marriage. Likewise, children are crying out inwardly and outwardly in some form for their parents to give them more time and to listen to them. One study revealed that a group of middle-income fathers claimed to spend twenty minutes a day in close contact and conversation with their one-year-old children. An attached microphone accurately revealed those fathers averaged talking only thirty-eight seconds a day to their children! [14]

A third-grade schoolteacher gave her students the opportunity to list what they disliked about their parents' bad habits. The recurring theme, written with the original spelling, is captured in this statement: "I wish my parents would cwit fusn and lisn to me and help me too. Oh yes, my dad can cwit smoking." [15] The teen years are important ones, but if society has directly and indirectly taught families to be too busy to listen to the children during the first eight years, the children's makeup is already determined! Most psychologists say that teenage shoplifting by middle- and upper-class children is done as an attempt to gain their parents' attention. Their parents give them everything they want—except themselves!

Some children hide their feelings of being ignored or rejected by their family without resorting to any noticeable extremes. But again, their anger and resentment may explode in an unusual way, either as a teenager or as an adult—like the bizarre rampage someone goes on and then is described by his neighbors and co-workers as the "ideal" person. A lesser form of explosion within may be the person who cannot decide what work he wants to do, who is always moving from one place to another, who is in and out of numerous marriages, or who batters his spouse and children. *Society cannot forever misuse the family without someday having to pay the price!*

A society that once knew genuine poverty has substituted their attempts to gain more and more in place of the one true God. When God is not in proper view and man is ignoring God's expectations, it becomes easier to forget, dilute, or reject God's intention for the family. In the name of economic growth, creature comforts and all the modern conveniences and recreational possibilities our society has become rich with things and impoverished before God. Only the totally spiritually blind person fails to see how utterly impoverished he stands before God. Most families have been so brainwashed by society they have stopped teaching their children that their first loyalty is to God and his will and in light of that commitment to establish their loyalties to family and others. Society teaches loyalty to the various and sundry peer groups with little or no room for God or the family.

The family came into being as the first institution of mankind, but unless some drastic changes are made in the last quarter of this century, the remaining strengths of the family may be washed down the drain. Every conceivable organization demands cooperation, participation, and support, leaving the family little or no time for nurture, dialogue, interaction, or intimate growth.

Fewer and fewer parents are fulfilling their responsibility of adequately caring for their children. That this is a fact is sad. But that many families have given up any attempt to alter this fact is even more tragic! Family life in the second half of the twentieth century is emotionally ragged and spiritually impoverished.

Like the freshman politician, the proverbial "volunteer," or the new employee, it appears the family is too frequently bowing to the pressures of pleasing everyone else in every way possible. Few families reserve even one night a week for family activities. Even fewer families consider it a priority to devote prime time to family discussion and interaction. But almost every family plans restaurant meals, shopping sprees, multiple leisure-time possibilities, and regular vacation trips. Peer pressure causes adults and children alike to keep on the move, keep up with peers, keep moving up the ladder, and keep away from honest, growing relationships within the family. Frequently the children of middle- and upper-class families are abandoned emotionally as much or more than ghetto children. The lives of the family members fail to interlock, leaving a vast sea of turbulent emotional space.

It still seems heartwarming to see a parent and a child holding hands. It still seems a beautiful expression of love to see a parent kiss his child. It still seems encouraging to see a family doing something together. But society is not teaching or encouraging these interactions. Adults, instead of being the models for the children, are now trying to appear like their children! Priorities of time and energy dissipate instead of binding up the family. Society seems to have forgotten that what strengthens the family ultimately builds a stronger society. The communist countries are now beginning to admit this fact and have laid aside old commitments and are reemphasizing family life. The jury is still out on society's misuse of the family in America. At this point, if the family grows stronger together and returns to God's intention, it will be the result of a *reaction to* instead of a *succumbing to* the pressures and practices of a society that misuses the potential of the family.

[1] Haim G. Ginott, *Between Parent and Child* (New York: Avon Books, 1969), p. 161.

[2] Trueblood, *The Recovery of Family Life,* pp. 13-15.

[3] Associated Press articles in *Concord Tribune,* June 5, 1978 and *The Charlotte Observer,* January 2, 1979; *New York Times* Special Feature, "The Last of the Housewives," Terry Martin Hekker, in *The Roanoke Times,* May 17, 1978.

[4] William Barclay, *A Spiritual Autobiography* (Grand Rapids: Wm. B. Eerdmans Publishing Company, 1975), p. 15.

[5] "Wife Beating Widespread, Study Says," *The Charlotte Observer,* June 28, 1977.

⁶ Celeste Loucks, "Child Abuse," *Home Missions,* September, 1978, p. 20 ff.; *Chicago Tribune* article, "Many Parents Violent with Kids," in *The Charlotte Observer,* February 26, 1977.

⁷ *The New York Times* article in *The Charlotte Observer,* June 5, 1978.

⁸ "A Letter Written By a Boy," *Pennsylvania Law Enforcement Journal,* quoted by Robert A. Raines, *Creative Brooding* (New York: The Macmillan Company, 1966), pp. 81-82.

⁹ Trueblood, *The Recovery of Family Life,* pp. 18-19.

¹⁰ Dr. Earl Schaefer, "Researcher Says Parents Are the Key," *Concord Tribune,* September 28, 1977.

¹¹ Craig, *Raising Your Child . . . ,* pp. 105-106.

¹² Herbert Hendin, "Religious Cults," *U. S. News & World Report,* June 14, 1976, p. 53.

¹³ "Are You Competent?" *The Charlotte Observer,* June 19, 1978.

¹⁴ James K. Page, Jr., "Phenomena, Comment, & Notes," *Smithsonian,* February, 1977, p. 13.

¹⁵ *Concord Tribune,* January 18, 1978.

3

The Potential of the Minister's Family

That the family is under stress and fire in the last quarter of the twentieth century is a conclusion no one will question. Some observers of our society have referred to the family as an endangered species. Only a few will doubt that the minister's family faces severe stress and pressure. If there is to be any hope for any family, including and beginning with the minister's family, it is important to take inventory of what benefits and potential the minister's family has. There are some unique traits of this family that can be enjoyed and appreciated once they are pinpointed and celebrated. At the same time, the potential of the minister's family can be ignored, creating a vacuum in the lives of the family members.

Thus far we have sought to understand God's intention for families and have observed some ways society has misused and abused God's intention. Now we look carefully at how the minister's family can be a bridge over the troubled waters of society's misuse of the family into the green pastures of God's intention for the family.

What are some of the unique benefits of the minister's family that afford it the opportunity to be a bridge in a troubled society? First, the minister's family can realize a unique opportunity to learn the full impact of God's love. The trained minister has the assets both of intense biblical learning and the study of human behavior. More than many other professional counterparts in society, the minister has the potential of engaging his family in the dynamic relationship between religion and psychology. Not that the family members are to become guinea pigs, but the minister has the background to provide an exciting environment for family growth.

More than one ancient interpreter has looked at the statement of Jesus in Matthew 18:19-20 as a beautiful affirmation of the family: ". . . Where two or three are gathered together in my name, there I am in the midst of them."

The minister's family has the potential to equip children to grow up and face the harsh realities of the world in the power and presence of the unseen enabler of God, the Holy Spirit.

A second benefit of the minister's family is an exciting dimension often overlooked. Few families have such a unique opportunity to know where and how the father/husband works as does the minister's family. Some men do exclusively secretive work, such as government intelligence or even highly competitive industrial research and development. Some men travel out of town almost every week and frequently for several weeks at a time. Some men are never able to take their family to see what they do or to describe adequately what they do. Indeed, some men would not want their family to observe their work! But the minister's family has the joy and opportunity of sharing in the father's work. It is an advantage, not a disadvantage, for children to know what the father does and to be able to observe him doing his work.

Granted, there are inherent problems in being so keenly aware of and involved in the father's work, but at the same time there can be a great deal of enjoyable sharing as a result of appreciating this unique profession. For example, a minister's child can appreciate knowing not just that "Daddy has to work tonight" but that "Daddy is helping some people who are sick" or that "Daddy is talking and praying with some people who are sad." Likewise, the children and wife will have numerous opportunities to meet and know people that perhaps they would not meet otherwise. This includes community leaders and international guests of the church as well as all the families in the church instead of just those who live in the neighborhood.

The minister's family can frequently travel and see interesting places in conjunction with conventions, conferences, and study trips. When the minister's expenses are paid, often the minister can pay the additional costs for his family to accompany him. Not only do they get to enjoy traveling and sight-seeing prior to the scheduled meetings, but also they can catch a firsthand glimpse of convention and conference proceedings.

Perhaps one of the most challenging benefits of the minister's family, in the third place, is that they have the potential of being a worthy model of family life for others to follow as they seek to pattern their lives after Jesus Christ. This is not to imply that any minister's family is perfect. But, a healthy sharing of the truths the minister and wife have learned through biblical study, prayer, and meditation can enable the minister's family to be a citadel of love and strength, and, in turn, a model for other families.

A real key is gaining the ability to apply in life the principles learned in study. This is in no way an attempt to endorse or perpetuate the "glasshouse syndrome." It is an honest declaration of the minister's family's need and opportunity to achieve all God intends for them. God has proclaimed his intention for the family, and if a minister is going to try to be an enabler of healthy Christian families, he begins with, includes, and always keeps coming back to his own family! The minister's family can internalize and demonstrate positive, hopeful, helpful, honest, challenging qualities. Just as the minister can live God's truths in his own family and in his larger community, so the minister's family can apply their truths both to their own existence and to their witness of Christian family living beyond their household.

Granted, the potential and unique benefits are present for the minister's family. But, close observation shows that often the benefits are ignored and the potential lost. Let us isolate a few of the ways the minister's family abdicates its uniqueness. One way the potential of the minister's family can be short-circuited is if the minister fails to support and understand his wife. Many ministers will stand up in their ministers' meetings and complain about the way the church members take their wives for granted. But at the same time, too many ministers expect their wives to always have the house straight, always hold the meals late, always stretch the budget, always keep the children straight, always attend the meetings, always be ready to entertain, always have a smile, always deal with unhappy members, always be supportive without ever giving them the physical, emotional, and spiritual support they need. Such expectations of any person, and particularly the wife and mother who is in the limelight and under pressure as the minister's wife is, are unrealistic and unhealthy. Undoubtedly many families fail to reach their potential because the minister fails to give his wife the consideration he urges his members to give one another! A great deal of the bitterness and resentment ministers' wives feel may be tied to the attitudes or rejection by church members, but may more likely be rooted in the casual way their husbands deal with their feelings and needs.

Naturally, such a failure in the husband-wife relationship snowballs and creates hostility, confusion, and failure in the parent-child relationship, and thus the potential of the minister's family is short-circuited again. Instead of using their rich opportunity for growth and development, more than a few minister's families experience heartbreak. Part of the problem can be traced to the method in which the children are reared. Children cannot be pushed to and fro and ignored at convenience and then be expected to behave well or grow in Christlike maturity. It was reported several years ago that one minister's son offered his father ten cents an hour to play with him! Some men are so busy trying to preach and teach righteous living they fail to take the time to show and explain the Christ way of life to their children.

The story is told by a social worker who found a little crippled boy by a ghetto tenement house. She investigated and learned the little boy had been run over by a truck several years earlier and never had received any medical attention. With enthusiastic determination, this social worker began the long process of helping this little boy. After two years of operations and therapy, he finally was able to walk straight without any assistance. He could even turn flips. The social worker proudly felt that if she never did anything else in her life, she could look back upon this singular accomplishment. She concluded the story by asking people to guess what the boy was doing some years later. After hearing everything from doctor to politician, she sadly replied he was serving a life sentence for committing the worse crime imaginable. She indicted herself by saying, "You see, I was so busy teaching him *how* to walk, I forgot to teach him *where* to walk." [1] It is a cop-out to teach only theory without giving the example, direction, and encouragement for Christlike living in the minister's home.

Perhaps one of the most severe cop-outs, and a third way of dissipating family potential, is for the minister to consider, or actually call, himself god. "Nonsense," you say. "What man could fall into that trap?" The man who elevates himself beyond question or reproach is guilty of such a cop-out. He is unavailable to his family while all his time and actions are devoted to activities completely "holy" and "righteous." A great many people read with sadness the report from Salt Lake City in the summer of 1978 in which a wife and seven children jumped to their deaths from a hotel window two days after the husband/father had committed suicide. This man, Immanuel David, had been a self-proclaimed god for several years. He had been supported by people who believed his extreme religious concepts and predictions of evil things that would happen. He and his family lived in total isolation from the world in a $90-a-day hotel suite into which $150 or more food was catered daily. By 1978 the religious enthusiasm of the early seventies had waned and his money supply was dwindling. The hold he had over his family left them no room to go on living. They followed his suicide with their own.

Few ministers commit literal suicide or drive their family members to do the same. However, the life-style chosen and lived by more than a few ministers shortens their life span, ruins their health, and dissipates the joy and potential of their families. Unfortunately some of the emotional and spiritual tragedies of ministers' children are spawned by the aloof, powerful, unloving, holy aura of self-righteous fathers. Children can see through the facade of their parents, and they resent having to uphold a "perfect" image of their father when they hear negative language and see negative behavior and attitudes in their home.

The minister's family need not be overwhelmed by these temptations to cop out. Instead, they can integrate some key values in order to survive and live up to their full potential in a unique, special home. The minister, his wife, and children need to be able to demonstrate a public commitment to marriage and the family. There need be no embarrassment or attempt to conceal the fact that the couple and/or family have a special day or evening for family time. Instead of succumbing to the cry of having to be the glasshouse family, there can be a genuine effort to celebrate privately and publicly the special gifts and opportunities that exist for family growth and enriching relationships.

The minister's family should support each other in genuine love. Where else is the message of love proclaimed more freely than from the lips of a minister? The words and concepts can be implemented in the home with even more effectiveness than in the church, for the level of trust and interpersonal relationships can be accentuated more readily.

Supportive love means giving children responsibilities appropriate to their age and helping them to grow and mature. Supportive love includes enabling children to understand what the real world is like so they can demonstrate sensitivity, tenderness, affection, and warmth both to their family members and to others who need these qualities. Supportive love means the parents discuss family matters with the children who are given the opportunity to help solve problems and resolve significant issues. Likewise, it means the children accept appropriate responsibilities and maintain their trust in and commitment to their parents who, under Christ, are seeking to lead the family in the Christ walk of life.

It might appear to be obvious without saying it, but the minister and wife need to take the time early in the lives of their children to help them realize the benefits of the minister's family. Blessed is the minister and wife who teach their children by word and action that theirs is a privilege and not a chore to be a minister's family! By talking with children at a young age, the parents can help them understand two things: They are responsible first and foremost to God, and secondly, they are responsible to each other within the family. If these two crucial factors are taken care of, their witness to the church as a family will be seen in proper perspective.

Ministers must ultimately ask themselves what will it profit them if they win the whole world to Christ and their own family goes to hell! The worse thing that can happen to any family, and most especially the minister's, is for a facade to develop that implies "all is well"; "everything takes care of itself"; and that there are no real needs or pressures within the inner sanctum of family life. Such a rose-colored front does nothing but increase tension and pressures within the family. Surely the area of greatest work for any minister is that within his own family. In his own home is the place for exemplifying love, compassion, tenderness, consistency, faithfulness, interest, attentiveness, sincerity, and thoroughness. A minister can and will teach his congregation a great deal about marriage and the family by the way he treats his own.

A minister's wife has a powerful influence on how the children will feel about Christian growth and the church through the attitude she exhibits. Children pick up more quickly and thoroughly on subtle nuances and inferences than many adults do. Children readily determine if their mother's heart and soul are in the work and ministry which demands so much of their father's time. Children who decide that the church and work are competitors for their father's attention will have a resulting indifference and/or hostility toward the church and all it stands for. Therefore, the wife who genuinely supports and participates in her husband's ministry not only is a help to him but also affects her children's appreciation of, understanding of, and maturation in the Christian faith. Children who are "raised not by force, but by love" will be better equipped and more willing to lovingly participate in their homes than those children who are disregarded, ignored, or manipulated. The minister and his wife are facilitators for developing Christian character and a sense of well-being in their children. By the help of God, they can help their children gain a sense of self-worth based on God's love for them and their parents' love for them.

The minister's family has unlimited potential! It is the warming oven in which growing relationships can be nurtured between husband and wife, parent and child, and the family and the church. It is also the place in which the congregation and larger community can look to discover the purpose God originally intended for the family. Though it may never achieve perfection, neither should it settle for mediocrity.

[1] John R. Claypool, "Providing and Preparing," Northminster Baptist Church, Jackson, Mississippi, June 19, 1977, p. 8.

PART 2

Introduction

In the first segment of this book, attention has been devoted to the family as it was intended to be, the family as it is in society, and the family as it could be in the minister's home. All of this may seem like little more than an unattainable ideal. And indeed it is, considering the manner in which many ministers and their families exist day by day!

There are quite a variety of reasons many parsonage families fail to reach God's ideal. The second portion of the book will sketch some of the commonplace sources of stress and seek to delineate the causes in such terms that you and your family can come to grips with who and where you are. Hopefully, you will be open to avenues for coping with the stress that so easily side-tracks your full and abundant living.

4

The Question of Education

A clever little tale about a palm tree and a gourd illumines a great truth for growing disciples today. A gourd wound itself around a lofty palm tree and in just a few short weeks had climbed to the very top of the tree. Arriving at the top, the newcomer said, "How old are you?" The palm tree said, "About a hundred years old." The smart little gourd retorted, "Well, look at me, in just a few weeks time I have grown as tall as you." Calmly, the palm replied, "I know that. Every summer of my life a gourd has climbed up around me just as proud as you are and just as short-lived as you will be."

There is a great truth in this whimsical tale. That which is long-lasting and strong has deep roots which require cultivation, nourishment, patience, and time. Though the gourd makes a quick, flashy growth, it just as quickly dies away. The minister who wants to have deep roots and strong branches to enable him to function well as God's spokesman needs to develop and cultivate his Christian discipleship. That requires education, study, and discipline.

Jesus told a parable about shallow, short-lived attempts to grow discipleship. He concluded by saying that quality living was realized only in receptive lives (Matt. 13:3-9). "For to him who has will more be given, and he will have abundance; but from him who has not, even what he has will be taken away" (v. 12).

Growth for the committed minister is not optional. How he will grow is optional. He can either be like a gourd, or he can be like a palm tree! Education can be the crucial factor in determining the difference.

There are at least four major components in the stress focused around the minister's education. These factors are attaining formal education/training, functioning without formal education/training, keeping abreast with theological and ecclesiastical, education/training, and maintaining the discipline of regular study. Due to the central importance of one's education, both related to his ability to perform and to his opportunities to work, close attention will be given to each element of educational stress.

Relatively few ministers have been able to come to grips with the need for theological education and attain it without a degree of real difficulty. There are so many aspects to formal education that time, money, and vocational direction are only some of the main stress factors to face. For example, a man who feels called to the ministry has to decide what education he will strive for, when he will enroll in school, which school he will attend, how long he will be enrolled, what cost he will be able to afford, and how the education will be financed.

Men who go straight from college to the seminary without a family may experience relatively little stress in this facet of their ministerial life. However, since World War II a rising percentage of male seminarians are married and many already have children. Therefore, not only does the minister have himself to think about, but also he must take into account how his educational process will affect his family. Decisions must be made involving the wife's work, a second and maybe third job for the husband, the children's care, and other facets involved in this educational endeavor. The cost must then be measured both in terms of dollars and cents and in terms of the price of his family's sacrifice in being uprooted and living under intense pressure; while perhaps both parents work in addition to the father's being enrolled in seminary. Another dimension involves the wife's desire for education and whether both partners can secure advance education at the same time.

Many men who did not go straight from college to the seminary back away from formal training because of the expense involved. Not so much the expense in terms of the fees in one of the denominational seminaries, but expense in terms of what it means to the family.

Again, there are men who have been out of school for several years who desire to return and work on an additional degree. All of the same factors just described have to be reckoned with by the minister and his family. If the need and motivation for the education are sound, then perhaps the family can properly justify the cost they will pay in the stress of being uprooted and pressured additionally for the duration of the degree program.

Some families have detected that ministers have used formal training as a means of escaping responsible work. That is, some men drag their feet through one or more programs to avoid going to work "in the field." At the same time, some men will seek to turn their backs on problems in their work, their families, or themselves by pulling up stakes and "going back to school." Additional education can be a means of retooling, redesigning one's skills, or coming to grips with one's personal, family, or vocational problems. However, a man must be honest with himself and his family in precisely what are his sources of motivation for education. Children and wife alike can resent being pulled apart merely to escape an unpleasant situation or merely to acquire a degree or title to further the minister's status or ego. Even after the degree is secured, there may still be many years of repaying debts incurred while attaining the education.

Men who respond to the call to the gospel ministry later in life or with a family, frequently feel the price to pay for formal training is too great. Their stress becomes one of trying to function without formal training. They may be working in a small church while still working a regular or part-time job. They may be in an area far removed from a school and thus find it hard to develop personally or to move to church positions with more challenge or opportunity.

There are basically two options available for the man who has received no basic theological education or training. One is to take advantage of some conferences each year that will help him to develop some basic skills and have a type of short-term education. There are a variety of conferences available through a number of denominations. These include continuing education conferences offered through seminaries, incorporating the resources and professors of the seminary along with guest lecturers. Most denominations also sponsor seminary extension classes. There are two ways of participating in these extension courses. One is to take the work by correspondence and the other is to enroll in a local class taught under the sponsorship and supervision of the seminaries of that respective denomination. Either option offers a challenging opportunity for a minister to develop some basic, essential skills.

Another opportunity for some short-term education is to enroll for some training events at a teaching hospital in the state where you are. Almost every state has a hospital that includes some clinical pastoral education, offering course work on varying schedules, including one day a week, a six-week course, a three-month course, or a year's internship. Depending on your proximity to the hospital and time available, you can enlist in a class to aid in the development of your pastoral skills.

Almost every denomination offers some type of workshops on national, state, and local levels for ministers on the field. If you plan your time and your financial resources your church provides you to obtain ministerial training, you can develop quite a few skills over a period of months. Three or four one-day conferences locally each year plus one or two two-day conferences in the state annually along with a week at a national conference center will consume relatively little time or finances, but they will greatly enhance your total ministry.

Clearly there are some means of learning and training on the field for the man who has no formal theological training. There is another option, and that is to enroll in a training school for intensive work. Also, a minister could consider enrolling in a course at a local or nearby college which will stimulate his mind and assist him in the discipline of study. A good course in literature, psychology, sociology, religion, philosophy, or history can be a source of challenge and help. Regardless of the thoroughness and seriousness with which one approaches the short-term educational opportunities, he must remember they are only stopgaps. A strong case is to be made for the intensive, in-depth, formal theological education. But, there are some additional options available for the minister seeking the basic training to enable him to implement his divine-given gifts.

One option is to work with the personnel committee or governing body of your church to obtain permission to enroll in classes offered in one-month units. Most seminaries are now offering terms in June, July, and January. Obviously this option will take longer, but frequently it can be done in conjunction with ongoing ministry and family stability. If you were granted a month's leave a year, perhaps every second or third year you might receive two months off for special study. The minister who takes seriously the opportunity for study will make a difference in his church, and the people will be more willing to be flexible and supportive in this undertaking.

For the minister who has not completed high school or college work, there are a number of possibilities. Class work in a local technical school or community college could enable him to obtain a high school equivalency diploma or to secure his college work. Some men opt to enroll in a special training school for older ministers without high school and/or college work. The advantage of this option is a man can complete a core of competent work in less years than securing high school, college, and seminary training. The disadvantage is there will be some vital training missing which the longer, more thorough route provides. Unquestionably, there are some competent professional schools, such as Clear Creek and Boyce School in Kentucky and Fruitland in North Carolina which have produced many fine ministers.

It is possible for a minister who finds himself in a church position without formal training to function, and to function on an improving level each year. Growth will not happen accidentally, but serious growth can take place with genuine effort on the part of the minister.

Every minister faces the quandry of keeping abreast with the new materials being written and new trends in theological thought. Just as a surgeon's techniques learned in medical school become dated within five to ten years, so the approach, theory, and information gained in seminary leave something to be desired after a decade on the field. There seem to be two large pools in which seminary graduates flow after their formal education. One is that group which draws on the notes from seminary classes, using the same ideas and concepts learned years before. When that information becomes stale and ineffective, the minister is ready to move on to "greener pastures," or what in reality might be interpreted, "another church that will put up with his seminary notes!" Whether or not one's church catches on, a minister who is repeating the same old materials and concepts year after year is going to lose his freshness and vitality. There are important reasons for keeping abreast with new theological training, including what it will mean to the mind and the spiritual edge of the minister.

The second pool of seminary graduates is comprised of those men who annually seek to have some intensive training events to enhance what they learned and open new avenues of knowledge and service. A wealth of options are open to the thoughtful, innovative student-for-life minister. One does not have to return to seminary or graduate school to enroll in another degree program to be engaged in vital learning for the rest of his career. Consider several of the key possibilities.

The short-term measures suggested in the section above constitute a primary means for the seminary graduate to keep up to date with his theological education and training. A combination of local, state, and national workshops will be both appreciated and financed by the local congregation when they are properly presented as occasions for honing one's "tools" for ministry.

Quite a number of additional training events are open to ministers. A variety of overseas travel programs include advanced training in the Mideast and Europe in particular. Other major enterprises include the Yokefellow movements, both in Indiana and California, with their annual conferences. Reuel Howe began the Institute for Advanced Pastoral Training in Michigan from which he has now retired and it continues to operate under other leadership. Dr. Howe presently operates an Island Oasis Training Center on St. Simons Island, Georgia. Gordon Cosby's congregation in Washington operates Wellspring, a retreat center. These are but a few examples of the type of training that has nationwide prominence and accessibility for the concerned, interested minister. It is possible to keep abreast, possibly alternating a continuing theological education program on a seminary campus one year with a major conference of national significance the same or the following year.

The area of ministerial education that may ultimately be the most difficult to achieve and maintain is that of private, personal, regular study by the minister. Maintaining a regular, disciplined study on one's own is difficult but necessary. Anyone who has tried realizes it is easier to study when you go out of town for a conference and when you enroll in school and have the pressure of professors and classes to accomplish the required work. But in the final analysis, the educational depth and effectiveness of a minister is revealed in the quality and quantity of personally motivated study one does week after week.

One of the complex aspects of the minister's work is the broad field of study in which he is involved. While most other fields, professional and nonprofessional alike, consist of one major area of focus, the minister has a number of areas in which to maintain more than a casual acquaintance. For example, he should be well-versed in Bible study and interpretation, in theological understanding, in ethical values, in psychological concepts, in denominational emphases, in administrative insights, in teaching principles, in devotional exercises, in counseling techniques, in inspirational preaching, in innovative worship, in church organization, and in staff and lay supervision.

Certainly no one minister can be all things to all people, but a serious student of Jesus Christ can seek to maintain regular study hours that will allow him to work in a variety of areas in the course of a year. Each week should include regular Bible study and devotional time. The approaches and possibilities in this area are about as numerous as the denominations in the United States! A minister has only to choose the plan that is interesting and challenging to him, and to realize he will probably need to alter it every year or so. Certainly the study of the Scripture will be enhanced if you are continuing or beginning the study and reading of the original languages. But if you are not proficient enough now, do not rule out the possibility of reading the words that were initially written. And meanwhile, make good use of the best critical and devotional works on the Scripture passages at hand. Note the combination—the best critical and devotional resources—so that you neither miss the best of theological scholarship or the best of spiritual inspiration! Do not rely on one to carry you through completely, but learn to balance the two together.

A minister also needs to devote time weekly to the study and interpretation of current events, all the way from the international affairs to national politics and local concerns. No minister will realize where the needs or problems are in his membership unless he is keeping abreast with business affairs, political struggles, and local issues such as school busing, local taxes and zoning, and the interworkings or conflicts between the city and county government.

In addition to Bible study, devotional reading, and updated views of current events, a minister needs to keep in contact with the world of literature. From the classical novel to the best-seller, from poetry to prose, from the historical work to the biography, from the classical play to the contemporary drama, there is much to be learned from reading. The values and feelings of people are often times succinctly illustrated by the secular author. Information and inspiration can be gleaned and noted for reference, thereby expanding one's mind and enlarging the resource materials for preaching and teaching.

Another core area a minister must stay in touch with on a less frequent, perhaps rotating, basis includes subjects such as psychology, theology, ethics, philosophy, preaching, worship, religious education, and psychology. If no more than a book or two a year, or a week or two a year, is devoted to each of these areas, at least some concentrated effort will be devoted to maintaining an interest and fresh awareness of these vital arenas of information.

Professional journals can be one of the best sources for keeping abreast in current writing that can be incorporated in personal study. Seminary journals from across the nation, coupled with denominational magazines, are a beginning place. Other professional journals which focus on each of the above and other areas of study enlarge the wide range of possibilities you can draw upon for your personal subscriptions. If you are fortunate enough to live near a university or seminary, you might do your journal reading in a library.

Obviously there is a great deal of time involved in an ongoing serious effort at study and learning. There is never enough time to do all one needs to do and the temptation lurks nearby to brush study aside for "people-oriented," "result-producing," "more visible," contacts and programs. As grave as the temptation may be, every minister needs to realize he will not, cannot long be effective without regular, definite, specific study! Each man must devise his own schedule for studying. And as soon as he does, his family and his church needs to be informed of his study hours. Quite seriously, almost everyone will work to protect your time when they realize the difference that studying is making in your ministry!

Early in this chapter reference was made to the cost involved in theological education and training. This is a vital point many churches do not realize or understand. They do not stop to consider the number of years a minister is involved in study, years that he is neither gaining equity, building up seniority, or tucking away savings. Instead, he is only managing to survive, while frequently going into debt. Quite often a number of years following seminary are required to liquidate those debts because, unlike other professionals, the salary of ministers does not immediately jump to a high level. There is no big "bonus" to offset the educational costs.

There is also a continuing cost for the yearly education of the minister. Fortunately more and more churches are beginning to realize this fact and are budgeting not as salary or benefits, but as "tools," the costs entailed in continuing education, books, and journals needed for the growing minister. Hopefully the time is not far removed when churches will offer an extended study leave for competent ministers. Quite honestly, the results would benefit both the church and the minister. Certainly there would be more sustained work done in the same church if the minister could have a break. Unfortunately, a great many "church moves" come out of weariness and being so far behind the minister can no longer see "the light at the end of the tunnel." More than a few churches are granting a month, a year, or several months after five or seven years and are paying the costs, including those for overseas educational events.

If your church is not aware of your needs or costs for education, you might request the state office of your denomination to write several of your key lay leaders to share some information and inspiration with them on this topic. They will be glad to facilitate your further training.

No person in today's society can excuse himself for not sharpening his skills and learning new techniques. Resources are readily and easily available. The minister who takes seriously God's call to Christian leadership will find ways to be a good spokesman for God. "Study to shew thyself approved unto God, a workman that needeth not to be ashamed, rightly dividing the word of truth" (2 Tim. 2:15, KJV).

5

To Move or Not to Move?

Ours is a mobile society. Many people have come to take it for granted. But not many families, especially those in which the man has professional training, expect to move numerous times during the working career. Yet, the minister and his family continue to be often on the move, perhaps too often, in fact, for the health and well-being of the man of God and his family.

Nearly half of the average church family has close relatives living in the city or county in which they reside. Seldom does a minister live within a hundred miles of either his family or his wife's family. As a result they do not have the opportunity to enjoy the companionship of their parents—especially since they do not have any "long weekends" to go visit them! Even more, the children who grow up in the parsonage can miss the blessing of knowing and relating closely to grandparents, aunts, uncles, as well as cousins and all the other extended family. The advice, counsel, conversations, and shared love as well as the "inexpensive" baby-sitting and help with house chores and personal problems are all absent from the vast majority of ministers' homes due to the distance away from the family.

There is another facet of the mobility syndrome that differs from other professional families, and that is the job insecurity that plagues the minister. Even though only a relatively few churches extend an "annual call," there is still a great deal of stress on a minister to perform or feel the pressure to move on someplace else. Of course, the fact that the average tenure of a staff member in one of the largest denominations in the United States is less than twenty-two months is not a total reflection on the churches involved. In some instances it is indicative of the lack of training and the restlessness of the ministers!

A minister has a lot of people to please in order to "keep his job." There are so many intangible as well as tangible measuring rods that he must adhere to, including the measuring sticks of "growth" that are usually translated in terms of new members and dollars received. Unfortunately, many churches are blind to measuring the quality of their ministers in terms of lives changed, spiritual growth precipitated, inspiration imparted, marriages redeemed, souls transformed by Christ, vocational models held forth, seed sown, values aligned with Christ's, lives saved, desperation relieved, dreams implanted.

Due to the lack of sensitivity on the part of churches to the work being done by a genuinely dedicated minister, often good men feel forced to resign and move on. And it usually does not take more than one or two pressured resignations to cause a good man to "call it quits" with the professional ministry of the church.

The insecurity-mobility in the ministry certainly feeds the workaholism that fuels the machinery of many ministers. A man who always feels he has to prove himself in order to justify his present compensation—much less a merit increase—will always be on the defensive and always be trying to "overwork" for appearance' sake. The men who fail to see the fallacies of falling into this rut frequently fail to develop and use their best abilities while seeking to "be all things to all people" and keep their jobs.

Ministers also feel the stress of wondering if they stay too long that maybe no one else will want them. This is a very real feeling that sets in during the passage of the forties, both due to the feelings within the minister and the attitude of society in general. How often a church member or even the committee seeking to bring a minister to a church is overheard to say they want someone under forty or forty-five "in order to appeal to the young people." Instead of feeling that the best years of his ministry are to be given in his fifties and sixties, a minister frequently feels he must make a "strategic" move by the time he is forty to assure he will be in the best possible place. And, of course, if you follow on out the attitudes of many churches, that minister will not be able to move easily after age fifty-five to sixty, and his church may well feel he has stayed too long, is too old, and they must get a "young" man the next time! Such attitudes are a vicious part of the mobility cycle many ministers feel.

Another facet of society that confuses ministers and adds stress is the notion that "bigger is better." Therefore some ministers feel they must move up in order to improve their lot. It may be true that some churches are so small their outlook, program, witness, ministry, and potential may inhibit a minister's creative abilities and God-given gifts. At the same time there are many good, small, creative churches that need competent ministers to help them more fully live out God's plan for their corporate life. Likewise, there are many men who feel good about their ministry in a smaller church, while at the same time they feel the peer pressure and society's expectation to "move on up." It often takes some men several years and an unfortunate church experience to realize that "bigger" is not necessarily "better," and that society's expectations do not equal God's will!

Denominations in which the minister deals directly with a prospective church he might serve reveal that one of the major sources of mobility stress is that a minister might be unable to move when he wants to move! Some ministers feel hemmed in by their present circumstances. Some men feel their opportunities for creativity, effectiveness, and growth are inhibited and thus want to relocate. Other men desire a different size congregation and staff—most of the time larger—though some men are honestly seeing desirable advantages in working with a smaller parish. Whatever the feeling, when a minister has to depend on being recommended by a friend or denominational worker to another church and that "other church" is slow to appear and make its request of the minister, the stress factor really enlarges! Sometimes it is hard to remember the timetable God works on, and thus be patient. By the same token, it is difficult to realize that not all churches are sensitive to God's leadership, and therefore some churches may pass by a minister for various unfair reasons when God would use that minister well in that church's particular set of circumstances. At best a man needs to bear in mind that God has not called him, prepared him, and used him in the past only now to ignore him and desert him! Seeming immobility does not last forever!

Almost the opposite stress comes when a pastor selection committee approaches a minister and tells him, "We need someone just like you," or "God has led us to you," when all the while the minister does not feel God's leadership whatsoever! Charged by the church with the responsibility to go out and find the best man to enable the church to grow, many search committees become quite pious and aggressive in their attempts to sell their church and enlist the minister they desire. Unless a man is careful, he can be overcome with guilt for turning his back on such a tremendous need or such a compelling revelation of God according to the search committee. The fact of the matter may be that God has quite a different set of desires and intentions for that man at that particular juncture of his life.

Ministers need to cling to the knowledge that if God has spoken, both parties will know it! Several years ago in one denomination's national convention, an eloquent speaker got up to nominate a friend for the position of president of the convention, saying he had been led of God to make that nomination. Just as quickly as he finished his nominating speech, the man nominated came to the microphone to declare he had been prayerfully considering this possibility and God had revealed to him he should decline. Now unless God got confused, one of those men had missed his will, for God surely would not have made contradicting statements to two people on the same subject! There does need to be some room left for the possibility that a minister would not be entirely open to God's leadership being revealed through a search committee. At the outset of a committee's prevailing upon a man to come to their church, they may be entirely on target and the minister may be insensitive. But after careful, thoughtful prayer and consideration, if the minister still feels he is not led of God, he must be ready to refrain from moving, no matter how influential, impressive, or rewarding the position might be!

Certainly one of the most difficult aspects of ministerial relocation is the genuine stress of knowing and doing God's will. God does not always speak through the wind or the earthquake, as Elijah discovered. Frequently God speaks through a still, small voice—and that from an unexpected source. Often a person is best able to discern God's will in retrospect instead of at a given moment. Paul himself acknowledged that now we only know partially, but when we see Christ face-to-face we will know fully and understand everything (1 Cor. 13:12).

The minister who stays in tune with God's Spirit and is ready to serve wherever he feels God is leading will most of the time feel clear and definite about career changes. Each move might not be equally as clear as the first one or the last one, but each time God will give enough indication that a sensitive listener to God's holy whisper will be able to perceive what God is about in his life. An added plus comes when the minister and his wife are linked spiritually and are able to pray together about church moves. Then when both feel the same about making a move, there is the added certainty that God's will has been revealed and acknowledged.

Inflation has marched through our society at such a pace that more and more ministers are realizing not owning a house is a real liability. He neither has a means of gaining any equity in a home nor of securing a sense of permanence in a community. Likewise, there is no place for his family to live if he dies suddenly or early in life. Similarly, he and his wife have no retirement home.

Gradually in urban areas and even small towns there is a trend toward providing a housing allowance, enabling the minister to buy his own home, put down his own roots, pay his own taxes, and gain some security, both for the present and for the future. It is probably true that the only time to be given a housing allowance in lieu of a parsonage is when going to a new church. Well-intending though they may be, the search committee that says "later on" the church will provide a housing allowance neither has the power nor the interest to see through such a promise. The average church is quite content to keep a minister under the same living conditions that existed when he came to them. If a man has the desire to buy his own house and the environment offers a market for buying and selling a house, the time to establish such an arrangement with the church is at the beginning.

Often the family suffers more from the mobility of the minister's work than the minister himself does. Some men are not bothered by pulling up roots and starting over again. Indeed, as the last chapter on education pointed out, the men who did not secure a solid education or are not keeping up with improving their training find it more comfortable to move on when they run out of their bag of tricks.

On the other hand, the children can often be caught in an emotional whirlwind by never feeling secure with their friends or having to change schools in the middle of a year or the middle of a particular school. Likewise, with the growing percentage of working wives, some ministers' wives are quite disrupted in their career to have to make a move for the convenience of their husbands. Or, in the case of a woman minister, the husband is caught off balance when he has to make a move to suit his wife's new church position.

Mobility is not all negative for the family. A move can allow children to see and learn about a new part of the country, as well as to make a new set of friends. Just as a move can afford the minister the opportunity to start over and seek to eliminate some mistakes from the past, a move for the family can allow a child to be called by a different name, escape some stigma from the past, branch out into a new interest or hobby, or exert a new level of leadership or participation in school and/or church.

Moves that are made when a minister is tired, discouraged, or unduly pressured by the congregation can wind up with serious problems, hostility, bitterness, or regret on the part of the minister and his family. Surely the worse time to move is when a man is low emotionally, though that is the time one is most tempted to move! In a sense, moving to a church is like a marriage. No minister counsels a couple to marry quickly or marry on the rebound of another romance. It takes time and preparation to be ready to begin a good, lasting marriage. In a similar way, no minister should make a sudden move "on the rebound" from a bad, frustrating experience in a church, no matter how difficult it may have been. It takes some time to know one's own feelings and readiness to move into a church, just as it takes time to know and understand the needs and expectations of the church. If the marriage is going to be lasting and enjoyable, the time is well worth it!

The question "To move or not to move" can be either a source of stress in a minister's family or it can be a time of reaffirmation and recommitment to one's present circumstances. During times of mobility stress, it is wise to remember the counsel of Paul: "The peace that Christ gives is to guide you in the decisions you make; for it is to this peace that God has called you" (Col. 3:15, TEV).

One of the keys to coping with mobility stress is to discover and practice the fine art of living fully in the present. Work for Christ day by day. Enjoy your salvation day by day. Love your family members day by day. Serve others day by day. Grow in Christian graces day by day. Live today fully and allow God to take care of tomorrow.

When faced and used properly, mobility can be a friend instead of an enemy. The wise man of God learns to discern the difference.

6

Relating to the Household of Faith

The account is given of a minister whose family was in an uproar every Sunday morning. After five days of rising at the proper time, everyone getting off on schedule, and veritable calm and happiness in the early morning routine, everything came apart on Sunday mornings. The three children either misplaced their Sunday shoes or did not want to get up on time. Invariably there was a fuss or a complaint and then a spanking. The ride to Sunday School was comprised of an angry father, a weary mother, and at least one crying child. A minimum of one other child was "snubbing," that effort to stop the flow of tears.

One Sunday morning the minister and his family were leaving their driveway when they noticed the family next door in their yard. The father was sitting on the patio having his second cup of coffee while he was reading the newspaper. The mother was trimming her rose garden. The two sons were practicing lay-ups on their backyard basketball goal. The youngest child in the car, striving desperately to snub back the tears, looked at the family next door and said: "I . . . I wish . . . I wish we didn't have to go to church every Sunday." As soon as the desperate, weary mother heard him speak, she swung around and blurted out: "Shut up, don't you know that they are miserable?" [1] Funny, but so true! The minister's family can often be under such stress from a variety of causes that they make themselves miserable and miss the joy of their salvation.

Surely one of the primary stresses of the minister and his family is that of the "glasshouse syndrome." Regardless of how other members behave, they tend to expect a higher level of performance from the minister and his wife as well as his children. One recent survey of ministers showed those men ranked as the second hardest thing for them to do was to meet the requirements and expectations of their members.[2]

It is difficult to live with the double standard of pious church members. The deacon wants no one asking where his wife is on Sunday or Wednesday night, but he is the very first one to question the absence of the minister's wife unless she is in the hospital or one of the children is critically ill! It is tough to cope with the pressures adults place on the children of the parsonage. Ball practices on Wednesday night; work on Sunday morning; parties on Saturday night; popular movies, "PG" and "R"; fast driving in new cars; "sowing some wild oats"; may be normal routine for most other children of the church—except the minister's children! As though it is not enough to always be visible to and recognized by the church membership and larger community, the children feel the pressure of living up to expectations which may seem unfair.

The average minister approaches his work with the concept that he will try to please all of the people all of the time. The church has come to adopt and endorse this expectation as normal and reasonable. Because the wife and children are residents of the parsonage, they fall into the same category as the minister—they, too, are expected to please all the people all the time!

Paul offered some sound advice to the Roman Christians who were hung up on the issue of eating meat that had been used in pagan sacrifices. The mature Christians realized it was only meat that was well-cooked and inexpensive, and they saw no reason not to eat it. The weaker, immature Christians who had just abandoned their worship of pagan gods felt that to partake of meat used in pagan worship implicated them in the worship of those gods. Paul summarized in Romans 14:15: "If your brother is being injured by what you eat, you are no longer walking in love. Do not let what you eat cause the ruin of one for whom Christ died."

Paul emphasized that *where* the meat was cooked does not make it pure or impure, but he also said it was wrong to be a stumbling block to others by what one eats (vv. 20-21). We are not to live for the whims of others, for that would make us wind up serving men instead of Christ. But the minister's family should never lose sight of the fact that they can use the example and witness of their lives to help point others to Christ. The temptation is present to ignore or turn off those who have high expectations of the minister's family. Actually, this can be a ripe opportunity to give witness to the faith that lies within the lives of those redeemed ones who live in the parsonage. The minister and his family do have high expectations and they can use their position to an advantage to glorify God. But they must be careful not to try to live for others or make others' approval their god! It is to God and his expectations that the minister and his family must answer.

The minister's family, as well as any Christian, should never forget that because of their commitment to Christ, there are some expectations which not only are fair but are necessary and reasonable. The expectations of loyalty, honesty, winsomeness, faithfulness, and compassion are neither excessive nor out of reach. Very often Paul reminded his Christian brethren that they lived in a pagan, evil world and that their behavior must be completely contrary. Therefore in a world where envy, strife, immorality, jealousy, and anger are the components, Christian leaders need to hold high the banner of Christ which exemplifies love, joy, peace, patience, kindness, and self-control. (See Gal. 5:19-26, TEV.) The minister's family who views their expectations as positive means of witness will be freed of some of the negative connotations of the glasshouse syndrome.

Dealing with the multiple problems of the church membership adds extra stress for the minister and family. Those problems are as varied as unlocking the doors for a special group to helping a distraught family. Some people are reluctant to expose their problems to the minister whom they see regularly as worship leader, while others will call upon the minister at the slightest hint of a problem. Frequently the people who impose the greatest demands of the minister are those irregular or inactive members. And when a man is committed in the name of Christ to helping people who hurt, how can he refuse to go talk to the brother of a daughter-in-law who is presently an inactive member when the brother is an alcoholic who lost his job and is about to lose his family?

The minister is swamped with the routine problems of keeping a good, competent staff and supervising their work. Seldom do members realize how much agony and hard work goes on behind the scenes to produce newsletters, innovative and stimulating worship times, and other creative expressions of church life. Sometimes staff situations can cause stress. Some staff members are jealous. Some are not self-motivated. Sometimes a staff member is incompetent but hides undeveloped skills or inability well through apparent

busyness or manipulation of people's emotional support behind them. Occasionally a staff member is involved in sexual
immorality or financial dishonesty. No matter how wrong
a staff member might be and how airtight the case against
him may be, some people will still like and support that
person to the end. Those same people would bring condem-
nation to the minister who would be part of having the
accused staff member dismissed from the church.

The minister is faced with the problems of working with
lay volunteers who run hot and cold with the passing of
the seasons and programs. He has the difficulty of dealing
with people who may be inconsistent, inconsiderate, or incompetent in their jobs, and yet, he must be careful not
to offend these gracious, willing volunteers—the only army
he can muster!

The minister has the ongoing problems of the sick and
distressed, the aged and lonely, the doubting and bereaved,
the troubled, and those looking for handles for growth. He
has the problem of helping devise a church program that
will comfort the disturbed and disturb the comfortable. He
faces the problem of being involved in every facet of the
church while not wanting to make the church so dependent
on him that everything folds when he leaves.

Not only does the minister face problems in the church,
but also his wife and family do. Invariably the troubled
or distraught member who calls the house while he is studying or while he is away will wind up spilling all the frustration or concerns on his wife. She has to try to help the
member while attempting to shield and graciously defend
her husband. Her support is necessary and beneficial, but
who will support her emotionally while she is giving so
generously? Even the children's friends come to them with

problems, thinking that either they will have learned answers from their father or they can go to him and be anonymous help.

Dealing with one problem at a time poses no real stress. The real difficulty comes with the feeling that the parsonage is little more than a dumping ground for all the dirty laundry of the church and its extended family. This is the feeling that causes the minister to answer the phone with hesitation and causes his wife to go to the door with reluctance. Even when the family gets out of the house for a short while and goes to the shopping center or a restaurant, it seems that people see them and come with their problems even there. The amazing thing is that a person can dump an amazing, ugly situation in the minister's lap, and then walk away seemingly unhindered. Then the minister and/or his family have to dig out from under the wreckage of the emotional dumping.

Patching up hurt feelings takes a real toll on the minister and his family. Countless hours are spent in discussing strategy, personal visitation, talking on the telephone, and following up various conferences and encounters. Some of the most significant ministry a man does is in binding up the emotional wounds and spiritual gashes of his membership. The disgruntling part of it all comes when he has to seek to work out hurt feelings in an instance that no hurt was merited, or the hurt comes from misinformation or pettiness. Certainly a minister can cope with the stress of trying to soothe a potentially volatile situation, though if he recognizes it as a petty gripe of a demanding member the stress is made even greater. The ministerial study cited earlier in this chapter disclosed the three greatest causes of stress were lack of response to the minister's leadership, conflict within the congregation, and conflict between the minister and the congregation.[3]

Ultimately there is a limit to how much of this kind of stress a minister can suffer in silence. There is a fine line between "keeping the peace" and being a peacemaker. Sometimes one who is a peacemaker disturbs the peace in order to create it. Churches may become quite concerned about a minister who lights the match on any and every issue. But there are some occasions which demand the minister's leadership in getting some of the cobwebs cleared out of an ancient corner of the church's life. Stress is a part of such leadership.

Jesus never expressed anger toward persons as individuals, but he did show anger toward groups of people who were following mob psychology to commit injustices. He drove the moneychangers out of the Temple not because he was indignant at individuals but because he saw their collective action disrupting and destroying the spirit of the place people worshiped. Jesus disrupted the peace in an effort to make real peace. Any minister must be extremely careful when he chooses to pick a controversial issue and "disturb the comfortable" over it. If he handles it well, it may be one of the most crucial aspects of his ministry. If he mishandles it, it could be the beginning of the end of his ministry. At any and all times he must maintain the distinction between what must be protected and defended at all costs and what needs to be shaken up for the gospel's sake and for the sake of genuine, lasting peace.

One of the real dangers for a minister coping with church stress is to adopt subtly, perhaps unconsciously, the "Elijah complex." That is to say, a man comes to the place of feeling what he is doing is so important, how he is doing it is so genuine, why he is doing it is so divinely inspired, and where he is doing it is so right that God will not let anything happen to him. Just like Elijah, he feels that God will keep on using and blessing him until God finds someone else to wear his mantle. And even then, God will spare him the pain of death and will simply take him straight on to heaven!

This attitude of the minister may cause him to be unwise in his response to stress. Instead of being reasonable in the amount of church problems he tries to shoulder, he keeps taking everything that comes his way. Frequently the minister is blamed by the church for any and all weaknesses they are experiencing, and sometimes he may merit some of this kind of criticism if he is trying to be involved personally in every decision and every action of the church. Jesus demonstrated in his ministry time and again that he needed to be able to escape the stress of the people to whom he was ministering. At times he walked away from human need—emotional, spiritual, physical, and mental—in order to gain perspective and new strength for coping with that need. If our Lord himself could retreat momentarily so that he could regain his communion with his Father and be his best when he did minister, then surely the modern minister can do no less!

Little Trixie in the comic strip, "Hi and Lois," noticed how serious and solemn her parents became when the world news came on television. She left the room and went to a place where she could escape their sad faces and find relaxation. As she climbed into her favorite place, she said to herself that it really was unfortunate babies cannot talk because they would have solutions to all the problems of the world. The last frame of the strip pictured her sitting in her toy box surrounded by all her favorite toys. Wisely she declared that every adult should have a toy box where he could sit![4] Certainly every minister needs a place to go and escape some of the tension and release some of the pressure of the problems the church stress places on him. During times of stress, every minister should remember his call to the ministry as well as the *One* who called him.

Remembering the struggles of Christ's ministry should encourage and hearten the contemporary disciple. When feeling discouraged and defeated, hear the words of Jesus:

So you feel beaten, bullied, and whipped by the demands that people make on you, inconsiderate people who are so troubled that they can think of no one but themselves. Well, that's what you bargained for when you entered my ministry. And it is my ministry. Read about it in the Gospels. They tell you about a typical day in my earthly career, a day that begins, continues, and ends with crises, a day of involvement in human need, battling with human hypocrisy, a day that leaves me depleted, exhausted, and ready to quit—except that I find renewal in prayer. So why should it be any different for you, . . . ? A servant is not greater than his Lord.[5]

"Therefore seeing we have this ministry, as we have received mercy, we faint not" (2 Cor. 4:1, KJV).

---

[1] Bill Treadwell, "I Wonder Why They Seem So Miserable?" *The Winepress,* Vol. 6, No. 1, November, 1977, p. 3.

[2] "The Critical Personal Needs of Pastors," Kenneth E. Hayes, Project Analyst, Sunday School Board of the Southern Baptist Convention, June, 1976.

[3] *Ibid.*

[4] *Concord Tribune,* September 4, 1977.

[5] Leonard Griffith, *We Have This Ministry* (Waco: Word Books, Publishers, 1973), p. 16.

7

Balancing the Budget

Peter spoke up. "Look," he said, "we have left everything and followed you. What will we have?" (Matt. 19:27, TEV).

"He was shepherd and no mercenary."
(The Parson in Chaucer's *Canterbury Tales)*

In the United States the cost of living doubled between 1967 and 1978.

From the standpoint of practicality and necessity, the minister and his family must come to grips with their economic status. There is a tendency among ministers today to view their economic position as inadequate and often downgrading. Some feel their plight is unique to our present inflationary generation. But the pressures involving money have been present since the days of the first disciples. It was the rich young ruler's material wealth that blocked his acceptance of Christ's offer of superior wealth. When the times became confused, Peter reminded Christ of all they had forsaken in order to follow him. In secular literature down through the centuries the minister has been presented as a man of poverty, a condition expected of him by parishoners.

Today, for many ministerial families, the economic stress is one of the greatest sources of anxiety in the home. Apart from the denominations whose origins are in the European state churches, the religious movement in America had its beginnings with ministers who held secular employment in addition to their clerical duties. Not necessarily out of choice, but due to the sparsely populated areas and lack of funds, few of our spiritual forefathers were able to be "full-time" ministers. Of course, some of the more staunch individualists, such as the mountain ministers, were proud of the fact that they, like the apostle Paul, provided their income through secular means. Today, in many instances, ministers are among the poorest paid professionals. (By professionals, the writers mean those men who have professional training and whose actual work responsibilities are comparable to those of the lawyer, doctor, bank manager, or industrial manager.)

Questions arise: Is it wrong for a minister to want to be well-paid? Should a minister expect compensation equal to his professional peers? Should material lack automatically be considered part of the lot of the minister? How much is enough? These questions are important and necessary to ask. "The answer to our dilemma is not evasion or a sell-out to materialism, nor yet a divorce from the time and place in which we live. Rather *it is a frank acceptance of the tension.*" [1]

The real issue is how can the minister's family live in a world where "Money is king" without allowing it to become their king. After all, the minister's budget has needs common to all: housing, clothing, food, medical care, education, transportation, retirement, insurance, taxes.

Like any family, the real problem for the minister's family is keeping in perspective needs and wants. Taking into account our dependence on a highly industrialized and urbanized society, the minister's family, like any concerned Christian family, should be careful not to allow the world to "squeeze them into its own mold" of worshiping the money god.

When Jesus sent the seventy disciples out to witness, he told them not to carry provisions, because "the laborer deserves his wages" (Luke 10:7). Paul defended his practice of paying his own way through tentmaking in order that he would be indebted to no one. Then he went on to declare that "the Lord commanded that those who proclaim the gospel should get their living by the gospel" (1 Cor. 9:14).

Elsewhere Paul wrote: "for the scripture says, 'You shall not muzzle an ox when it is treading out the grain,' and 'The laborer deserves his wages' " (1 Tim. 5:18, citing verbatim Deut. 25:4 and Luke 10:7).

Clearly Jesus intended that those who prepare for the special equipping and enabling ministries of the church be paid a fair, decent, living wage. The fact this is not done by many congregations is a reflection not on their righteous use of the Lord's money but on their blindness to do what Jesus taught!

One of the reasons some ministers appear so mobile is that they cannot possibly live on the wage they are being paid and they feel they must move to a better paying position. This action brings up two questions: Was the Lord in the minister's going to the low paying church to begin with? Was the Lord leading the man to move to a higher paying position? The Lord does promise to see that our provisions are cared for, and surely he works through churches. Without a doubt some churches are deaf to the Lord's leading, while at the same time some ministers become too concerned about how much they are earning and how much they are saving. Each time a minister worries about his income, his concentration and effectiveness in his ministry are lessened.

Some of the physical and emotional ailments of ministers

may be attributed not just to strenuous work but to the worry over finances and future security. The majority of denominations still provide a parsonage/pastorium/manse in which the minister lives rent free. In days gone by, in which almost all the congregations were rural and no extra housing was available, this plan was not only workable, it was about the only feasible one! Even then, ministers who lived to retirement had no place to go. The emotional stress stemming from economic worries can be contributing factors in the development of high blood pressure, ulcers, and other ailments.

Society has changed in the last half of the twentieth century. Housing is more readily available in most areas. With the inflationary spiral initiated in the mid sixties, housing is almost the only means of keeping abreast with the rising cost of living. A minister who is given a housing allowance is able to build equity in that home. He has favorable tax breaks by receiving some of his compensation as housing allowance. And if he becomes disabled or retires, he knows he has a place. In the event he were to die, he has the security of knowing there is a home for his family. A minister without a house and not a large enough salary to set aside savings, much less keep up with the inflationary spiral, is a man under real stress.

The rising cost of education is a source of concern for most ministers' families. Due to a salary that often fails to keep abreast with the cost of living, it is difficult, if not impossible, to set aside a sizable amount for college education. Ministers want their children to have enough assistance to accompany their incentive to complete college and even graduate school and would like to contribute as much as possible to the funding of an educational program.

A related source of stress may be the cost of the minister's education. This factor is frequently in the picture for the man who pursues a doctoral degree early in his career, as well as for the man who returns to school after he and his family have been on the field. The church often overlooks the fact that while the average church member has been gaining seniority and benefits upon entering the job market following high school or college, the minister who earns a basic seminary degree has earned no seniority, no equity, and likely accumulated sizable debts in the process. The debts increase if advanced degrees are pursued. It is not unusual for the minister on a regular salary to have to spend five to ten years liquidating his educational debts.

A source of pressure for the entire family is the underlying feeling that each and every purchase in the parsonage must be justified in the eyes of the congregation. Whether it is the occasional needed outfit for the wife, the braces for a child's teeth, the new car to replace an old model, or the new suit for the minister, the minister's family is uneasy facing the comments that will inevitably be made by the church members. The fact is if the family did not shop wisely and frugally, it would have to do without a number of essentials. This stress is perhaps one of the most degrading pressures confronted in the glasshouse syndrome.

Yet another stress that affects the minister's family is deciding whether or not the wife will work. Sometimes it may be the only feasible solution to the financial plight of the family. Yet, there are some churches who do not like the fact that their minister's wife is employed outside the home. This pressure, added to the financial one, can create deep feelings of anxiety and worry.

Vacations are another facet of the economic stress felt by the minister. Frequently he cannot afford to take his family on a genuine vacation. He may pay their way and take his family along on a convention or conference trip. But, at best, there is little time for sight-seeing or family enjoyment. Many places and events could be enjoyed by the minister and his wife as well as his children, but he usually has to deny the possibilities due to a lack of funds.

There is probably not another professional who has to live with such pressure to "produce, or you won't get paid" as the minister feels. The average church member measures the "success" of a man's ministry in terms of dollars given to the church, number of new members, and size of Sunday morning attendance. A man who works in a church whose environment does not lend itself to rapid or even noticeable growth in these areas will feel the squeeze in a hurry. Not only do churches seldom give merit raises, but also they can decline offering any inflationary adjustment.

There are a number of factors contributing to the workaholic tendencies of the contemporary minister, but certainly near the top of the list is the pressure to prove his worth in order to be compensated, poorly though that may be! While comparable professionals are both higher paid and have much more time off the job, the minister continues to plug away at gaining a sense of worth and earning the compensation needed by his family.

There are few jobs today that have a public declaration of the salary and benefits paid. Some government jobs are public knowledge, but most of them pay several times the minister's compensation. The entire church not only knows all the minister makes, but they also subject the parsonage family to the humiliating pressure of having his compensation up for open discussion. Anyone who has any petty jealousy, pet peeve, hurt feelings, or cheap shot to take at a leader can enter into the free-for-all over the minister's salary and benefits. More than one minister has been so humiliated and frustrated after the budget process was completed that he felt like turning the increase back to the church!

A great many ministers worry about sickness, disability, and retirement because there are no provisions made by the church to cover these times. Frequently men have been forced to give up their church or at least take a second job in order to pay for hospital bills for themselves or their family members. Many ministers have felt the lonely hurt of having inadequate government checks when they have become disabled or retired. Today few employers omit from the total compensation package a first-rate medical plan, a disability policy, and a retirement program equivalent to 10 or 15 percent of the annual salary. Yet the average minister either receives nothing or only a token amount in these essential categories. And if his salary is low, he has nothing left over to invest himself. More than one minister's family has suffered intensely due to the lack of funds upon the early death or disability of the breadwinner. And many ministers have died bitter deaths in retirement because the churches they served did not care enough to provide adequate retirement income.

The economic stress precipitates a great deal of worry within the minister about his future. Housing upon retirement education for the children, money to cover medical costs, income in retirement, and other factors can nearly immobilize a man's fruitful ministry. Jesus recognized the human desire to have material security and a sense of permanence. So, he sought to reassure his disciples and to give them guidelines which would enable them to see all things in perspective. He told his followers that even the foxes had dens and birds their nests, but he did not have a place to call his own to lay his head (Matt. 8:20).

If Jesus had stopped with this insight, we would of all men be most miserable! But he went on to say elsewhere: "Do not be anxious about your life, what you shall eat or what you shall drink, nor about your body, what you shall put on" (Matt. 6:25). He said that God cares about the flowers of the field that bloom beautifully today and are gone tomorrow and he cares about the birds of the sky. They do not work like men, and yet God loves them and feeds them. And if God takes care of nature in this manner, then how much more he will care for his children!

This passage follows Jesus' statement that no man can serve two masters, for he will be able to love and follow only one. Man cannot serve God and at the same time serve money and what it buys. Jesus never taught that we should seek poverty but he did teach us about what is important in life. He taught us how to choose between the valuable and that which moths and rust will corrupt. His teachings and commitment to him as Lord assist the minister's family in balancing the budget in such a way that will glorify him.

Jesus' words of counsel offer encouragement and hope for the economically oppressed minister: "But seek first his kingdom and his righteousness, and all these things shall be yours as well. Therefore, do not be anxious about tomorrow, for tomorrow will be anxious for itself" (Matt. 6:33-34).

George Beverly Shea had always wanted to sing in the Metropolitan Opera in New York City. Just when he felt he would not have an opportunity, he received a contract to join that organization which promised him prestige and wealth. His mother was aware of his struggling with his final decision about his career. She laid on his piano the new words of a hymn written by Rhea F. Miller. When young Shea read them, he composed the tune. This song comprised the answer to his dilemma and the theme song of his life. He returned the opera contract unsigned and has used his voice to glorify his Savior around the world.

When we think of the world's scale of values, we are thus tempted. The boxer, the baseball player, the successful businessman, and others have their ratios far above the allowance offered to preachers. But remember, a Milton received only $50 for Paradise Lost, a Beethoven lost $100 in producing his Ninth Symphony, and Sir Ronald Ross, who discovered the secret of combating malaria, had to sell his papers in the eventide of life to provide modest comfort for himself and his wife. The ministry is a stewardship of the grace of God, and out of seeming limitation there is poetry, and without a fortune a preacher can enrich thousands and prepare them for the final audit. The minister is a fool in this realm as in others, but let him know that he need not covet any man's possessions, not even his library or his church or his stipend or his popularity, for, with our limited opportunities and slender resource, we can, under God, be wealthy in the spirit of the sacrifice of the cross.[2]

When the stresses of economics sap the strength and energy of the minister, he does well to remember the words of Peter who appealed to ministers: "be shepherds of the flock that God gave you and to take care of it willingly, as God wants you to, and not unwillingly. Do your work, not for mere pay, but from a real desire to serve. . . . be examples to the flock. And when the Chief Shepherd appears, you will receive the glorious crown which will never lose its brightness" (1 Pet. 5:2-4, TEV). Thanks be to God for that glorious promise!

[1] Daniel D. Walker, *The Human Problems of the Minister* (New York: Harper & Row, Publisher, 1960), p. 81.

[2] Ralph G. Turnbull, *A Minister's Obstacle* (Westwood, N. J.: Fleming H. Revell Company, 1966), p. 32.

8

Living with the Clock

In a University of Idaho study the following issue was raised for study: If one's life seems to lack meaning and purpose, that means one is probably working too hard, ignoring fun, pleasure, and enjoyment. Research demonstrated this opinion to be false. People with little or no purpose in life put the greatest emphasis on achievement, pleasure, and comfort, and they wind up in a self-defeating exercise. On the other hand, those persons who have a purpose in life tend to be better adjusted, more competent, and derive more pleasure from life.[1]

Ministers who have purpose and meaning in their work potentially have the opportunity for a well-adjusted, competent, happy life. The fact that the minister works a great deal is not as detrimental as the fact that he is under such pressure in his use of time. When a minister fails to use his time to achieve all the things he feels are important, he loses the sense of happiness and meaning in his work. And more than likely, not only are the juices squeezed from his life, but also his family suffers the consequences of his life-style.

To some degree the minister is in charge of his schedule. He determines the shape of his study time, his prayer and devotional time, his office time, his counseling time, and his meeting time. At the same time the minister frequently lacks control over the events that occur which demand his time and attention.

In her novel, *The Steep Ascent,* Anne Morrow Lindbergh describes one person's feverish attempt to rescue time from its frantic race.

Many ministers know the agony of racing against time in order to complete their work. The wolves of time snap at their heels as they hurry from one task to another and the harried minister seeks relief. Of all modern professionals, the minister is just about the last one who makes house calls and is on twenty-four hour duty. Doctors, lawyers, bankers, counselors, and executives do their work with people who come to their office during regular hours. The night and weekend work is usually shared with associates, sometimes as few as two or as many as ten or more. The minister seldom has the luxury of being "off duty," regardless of other ministers who may be on the church's staff. Almost without exception, in a time of emergency the member wants to be seen by "the" minister and the minister, in turn, wants to share in the crises of members' lives.

As indicated in an earlier chapter, men who feel the need to justify their earnings will fall prey to the pressure to be all things to all people. Consciously, or perhaps subconsciously, such a minister is trying to earn and command a larger salary based on the number of services and favors he performs. A minister who is wrapped up in workaholism will merit the praise of the congregation who frequently will praise his hyperactivity all the way to his early grave!

Some churches spell out to their minister that they expect him to work five days a week. There are many ministers who will stay away from their office but will continue to make appearances to register favorable impressions. On the other hand, there are men who genuinely desire to have some time away from work but simply find it impossible when they are in town. The telephone does not stop ringing.

The requests and demands do not terminate, even though the minister is seeking to rest and renew himself. More than a few men have concluded they will have to get out of town in order to have an uninterrupted day off from work. This need is one that the church can be reminded of so they can do their part in seeking to enable the minister to break the work routine. Few members will verbally say they want their minister to work all the time. Indeed, many concerned church members who have seen ministers lose their health while working in their church sincerely want their minister to get away from work.

The odd schedule of the average minister compounds the pressure on his time. He is confronted with the need for time to study, time to work with the church staff and/or lay leaders, time to visit the hospitals, time to make visits in homes, time to work with committees, and time to do counseling. Frequently this work must be done at night at the convenience of the lay members involved. Certainly work such as weddings and funerals demand a large investment of time that must be scheduled according to the demand of those events. The funeral is immediately demanding, while the wedding is scheduled in advance. But each takes a great deal of time and effort on the part of the minister.

Many factors converge making it quite difficult for the average minister to take all the vacation promised him by his church. Church meetings and wedding schedules can consume most of the time his children are out of school. Often if the minister has not determined six months to a year ahead when he wants to be away for personal time, all the available days will become scheduled. Money is often unavailable for a vacation trip of any dimension. Work that needs to be done and members that need to be impressed tempt the minister to stay on the job year-round. Even getting out of town does not assure the minister will have his free time. More than one minister has returned home from a shortened vacation to attend to an emergency or crisis. Sometimes a brief vacation can be unnecessarily interrupted as in the case of a tired ministerial family who decided to "slip away" to a neighboring city for an overnight respite. That short period was interrupted by a phone call from a staff member reporting on a member who had entered the hospital for a routine checkup! Such a message was neither critical nor of an emergency nature. It could have waited a few more hours until the minister returned home. Even those brief hours could not be called their own!

At the same time, it is important to remember that the minister's family does not have a monopoly on disrupted plans. Other professionals and those in service professions (utilities, plumbing, heating) also know what it is to be called for emergencies. But certainly the entire family can come to feel frustrated when their occasional times away from the routine pressure is disrupted, or maybe even dissolved altogether. Great care needs to be taken that the minister and wife, in their weariness, not pass along hostile or angry feelings to their children. Such times of interruption should be dealt with honestly and openly, remembering that images and attitudes concerning the church are formed and embellished during such reactions to stress.

The minister gets no weekends off like his members! Even on holidays granted the minister by the church, he is seldom able to have the time or money to journey to visit with his family. As long as he has children in school, his time is quite confined. When the children are doing good work and the school officials will cooperate, the minister's best option may be to take the children out of school and do several days of vacation during a school week. This will normally work well if the children are able to do some significant sight-seeing while away from school.

Ultimately a minister has to stop and take inventory of his use of time. Unless he is careful, the one area of his life that will suffer the most in the time squeeze is his family. A Chicago newswriter reported on a study that disclosed infants "who are neglected in situations or by parents are likely to grow up retarded, emotional cripples." [2] How many parsonage children are there who are emotionally crippled due to the lack of time and attention from their minister-father? It is not enough to say that all men are busy and have little time with their children. It is a sad indictment on the quality and quantity of time spent with children when 44 percent of one group of children surveyed said they preferred "TV over Daddy."

Los Angeles police investigator Lloyd Martin reported some astounding facts and statistics on child pornography. He cited one producer of pornographic pictures and films who declared: "Let me tell you about kids involved in child pornography. They are children of lawyers, doctors, policemen, preachers—who are attracted to older men because their fathers have no time for them. They are searching for a father. And no one jumps in front of a camera for money. These kids do it for ego." [3]

Part of the problem with parsonage children is the attitude they feel when they are asking for their father's attention. The minister whose mind is constantly preoccupied with his work is little fun to be around. The minister who is trying to do all things for all people has to let down some place—and his family is the most likely candidate for the release of his frustration. The minister who comes home dead tired from mental and emotional work may be unwilling to concentrate on relating as a father to his children.

The minister who feels what he is doing or thinking is always more important than anything his children might contribute will always precipitate negative feelings within his children.

Children so desperately want someone to listen, someone to show they care, someone to affirm them, someone to give them some time.

Ditto, the young boy in the cartoon strip, "Hi and Lois," came home from school one day thrilled beyond words with some news he had to share. When he entered the house and spoke to his father, Hi turned him aside saying he was on the phone. Ditto then went into the kitchen to speak to his mother, and Lois sent him out saying she was mixing a recipe. Ditto went to his older brother's room, only to be yelled at and told to get out when music was being practiced with older friends. Ditto finally went to his sister who called through a closed door to say she was taking a bath. Later Hi and Lois looked out in the yard at Ditto standing talking in front of a big tree. Hi commented that Ditto was talking to a tree again. This was the same father who was encountered by Ditto on another day when Ditto asked him to play ball. Hi told Ditto he had a hundred things to do. With a long face, the young son asked if he could be the 101st thing his father had to do!

A minister has no control over a great deal of his time. But he can consciously work to guard some time for himself as well as some time for his family. He can leave some other good things undone so that he can do something good for and something good with his family. The man who refuses to devote time to his children is wasting his potential, no matter how much good he does otherwise.

No man can do all that could be done. Some time must be consciously budgeted and conserved for the minister's family.

You need not wait until you get to the end of your life, until you have a nervous breakdown, until you resign your church in weariness, or until your child's life is wasted.

You can begin now to cope with the stress of time and salvage some quality time, not just the leftovers, for the sake of your life, your health, your strength, and your family.

Weariness is part of the fabric of the ministerial life. Yet, we are not without aid in dealing with the stresses of time.

> Don't you know? Haven't you heard?
> The Lord is the everlasting God;
> he created all the world.
> He never grows tired or weary.
> No one understands his thoughts.
> He strengthens those who are weak and tired.
> Even those who are young grow weak;
>   young men can fall exhausted.
> But those who trust in the Lord for help
>   will find their strength renewed.
> They will rise on wings like eagles;
>   they will run and not get weary;
>   they will walk and not grow weak (Isa. 40:28-31, TEV).

That is good news for a rushed, weary family!

[1] John E. Gibson, "Measuring the Purpose in Your Life," *Family Weekly,* October 23, 1977, p. 18.

[2] Donna Joy Newman, "You Can Have a Heart-to-Heart with Your Baby," *Charlotte Observer,* August 14, 1977.

[3] Robert Sam Anson, "Pornography's Newest Victims," *Conservative Digest,* September, 1977, p. 29.

9

The Arm of Friendship

A minister once confided that following a move to a new church he felt very lonely. On the surface that would appear strange, for after all, the minister in a new church is the one person everyone knows by name and he is singled out for special attention. It would seem that a minister in the midst of a loving church congregation would never be lonely.

This very attitude constitutes the crux of one of the major stresses facing the minister and his family. Loneliness is not rooted in an absence of people. Loneliness comes about because of the lack of significant relationships with valued persons. Many ministers and minister's wives find it difficult to bridge the lonely gap of relationships. Again, one must be careful to make the distinction between being around a lot of people and being in close fellowship with some of the significant people in one's life.

A great number of the people encountered by the parsonage family are one-way relationships. That is to say, a person or family with a problem comes to the minister and/or his family. The troubled family comes not for what it can give but for what it can receive. And once its needs have been met, it is ready to move on, giving little or no thought to the needs of the minister's family.

More than a few people relate to the minister in a manipulative manner. Their intent in being near him or having a "friendship" with him is based on what they hope to derive for themselves. With the appearance of helping and supporting the minister, they are only seeking to feather their own nest of power, influence, and popularity. And when it comes down to a crucial decision, they seek to use their "friendship" to influence the minister in line with their way of thinking.

It is true that in many relationships the parsonage family experiences the feeling of being drained! When there is mostly "give" and little "receive," the tendency to feel overdrawn is quite real. This is true both for the minister and for his family—but to some degree, even more so for his family. The minister does receive some affirmation and adulation by virtue of his being in the public eye and in front of the public doors. His family, on the other hand, may go for days or weeks without receiving any direct personal loving words of understanding and affirmation from anyone in the church. One minister's wife shared how rich were the blessings she received when in public prayers members prayed for her and her family, as well as her husband. It may seem a small thing to many, but it was an act of affirmation and loving support for his wife.

This matter of social contacts has a great deal of hidden stress. People claim they do not want to "bother" the parsonage family so they do not come by for visits; they do not extend invitations to go out; they do not call to check on the family members; they do not use special occasions to express appreciation. But all the while the congregation is supposedly trying to "protect" the minister and his family, there is a lonely dry rot taking place within the parsonage! Admittedly, in a church of 300 families or more, not every family could drop by on a frequent basis. However, the families who really care could call to see if it were convenient to come by, or at least extend a personal invitation for an outing. Putting your feet under the same table with someone helps to dissolve the feelings of estrangement. Spending some time "eyeball-to-eyeball" can evaporate barriers and bridge the way to meaningful relationships.

The very same congregation that will literally abandon the minister's family in the parsonage may well turn around and expect them to be present for all the official social functions of the church and its numerous organizations. It is nice to be invited to a class social or a mission circle luncheon. However, in a larger church these social events can be very time-consuming when they are "pushed down the throat" of the minister's family. The lack of an invitation would hurt, but the freedom to say no is a real gift a church can give the minister's family!

The set of expectations the church has for the parsonage family colors to a great extent the flow of social relationships. Too little contact or the pressure for too much formal or casual group contacts can be very draining. The church that expects the minister and his family to have normal friends is a healthy church that enables the minister and his family to enjoy social and personal growth. Where does the minister's family go to develop friendships? How can they discover persons to meet the need for close friendships?

In 1976, two surveys were made by the Research Services Department of the Southern Baptist Convention's Sunday School Board. One was a survey of ministers' wives and the other was of ministers. It was interesting to note that the wives had more of their closest friends outside the church than within its membership, while the ministers reported they had more close friends within the church membership than any other group, including former church members and fellow ministers.[1] Only a very few of the respondants said they had no friends. Contrary to the rule of thumb of former generations, it is generally acceptable for the minister's family to have some genuine friends within the congregation. The only hitch comes when there is manipulation involved by either party—the members who try to sway the minister or the minister who tries to gain favors through the members.

Carlyle Marney once commented that he knew two groups of people within the church. One was comprised of the balcony people he picked out with which to enjoy sharing relationships. The other group was the cellar people who were given him! The minister and his family must be careful not to be overwhelmed or turned off by the shallow friendships thrust on them so that they fail to cultivate the persons who would be genuine, lasting, meaningful friends.

One facet of the stress produced by so many casual social contacts is the amount of time it takes the minister away from his family, or at times, the minister and his wife away from their children. It is a real delight when the entire family can be included for a meal, an outing, or some form of entertainment, either with the casual relationships and especially with the genuine friends. Of course, the genuine friends pick up on this fact and involve the family also.

When there are young children in the parsonage, it is nice when church members are willing to come to the parsonage, thus eliminating the cost of a sitter and enabling the children to maintain their regular routine. For any minister's family, it can be a real treat to have members come by for a visit. Social and spiritual discussions can transpire without the minister having to go out another night or be away from his family again. One minister's family experienced great blessing when some friends asked to come for a visit and then arrived with delectable goodies to share for an evening of fellowship.

The minister's family who is unable to find or is uncomfortable in finding close friends within the church can certainly turn to neighbors, fellow ministers' families, or professional colleagues within the area. Indeed, while it is good to have some church members who are friends, it is important to develop good friends outside the membership as well. This provides some shelter from any criticism of a clique and it gives stimulation from persons outside those who are aware of and sharing in the church with its multiple pressures and problems.

The minister and his family have the legitimate need of every human being—that is, to be accepted for who they are as individuals, and not for what they do. A lot of the expected attendance at wedding rehearsal dinners or Sunday School class functions is not based on the deep feelings of acceptance and appreciation as persons, but because the minister is the man who performs the wedding or preaches on Sunday. Certainly it is fine to be recognized for what one does, and it would be hurtful to be ignored at such obvious social occasions. But the point is the minister and his family could be so much more relaxed and able to enjoy the interchange more fully if they felt they were known, loved, appreciated, and accepted for who they are as unique individuals!

Jesus had an interesting balance in his life. He went to weddings. He had twelve close associates, and among them had three close friends. He had friends outside this group, such as Mary, Martha, and Lazarus. He related to people en masse and yet he dealt with each person who came to him as an individual. He seemed to be able to accomplish this varied set of relationships by staying in touch with his needs. Matthew 14 relates one of the times Jesus sought some time apart to deal with his loneliness. Jesus got into a boat to go out from the people for a while. They followed him. So he taught them and healed them. Finally he fed the multitude, numbering 5,000 men. For a second time on the same day he sought to be alone, sending his disciples on across the lake. When he came to them late that night, they were in a storm on the lake. Jesus surprised them both by coming on the water and by calming the storm. He was able to do what he did because of his time with his Father and his time of getting in touch with who he was.

Years ago someone said that a person who is always available will not be worth much when he is! It is a hard lesson for many ministers and families to learn, but every individual and family do need time alone. The minister who has learned to say no will be able to keep his social relationships in proper perspective. The minister who has laid aside the tempting pressure to meet all the expectations of all the people, all the time will be free to enter fully into those relationships he does choose. The minister who is genuine and authentic, hiding neither his weaknesses nor his needs, will ultimately be acknowledged by most people as genuine. And meanwhile he will be able to enjoy living with himself whether or not others affirm him.

Jesus' friends did not always understand or fully support him. Yet he was encouraged and uplifted by their presence and concern. The love he received from God for all mankind enabled him to feel deep compassion for the multitudes, who, in their blindness, were rejecting and even crucifying him. Matthew 23 records the series of woes he pronounced on the hypocritical scribes and Pharisees and at the conclusion of the chapter Jesus is expressing one of the most tender, compassionate statements in the New Testament. "O Jerusalem, Jerusalem, killing the prophets and stoning those who are sent to you! How often would I have gathered your children together as a hen gathers her brood under her wings, and you would not!" (23:37). Jesus' compassion on the multitudes was heightened and revealed through his care for and relationship with his friends.

Upon looking back on the gospel narrative, it seems absurd that Jesus would not have had any close friends for fear of upsetting the larger crowd. Likewise, the minister and his family need to stop and take inventory as to why they are hesitant to establish close, nurturing friendships. When a storm blows through the forest, one strong tree is blown against another that helps to support it. Together they withstand the tempest. And so it is with genuine friendships. A compassionate Christian caring with mutual uplifting is the real meaning of friendship. "A faithful friend is a sturdy shelter: he that has found one has found a treasure" (Ecclesiasticus 6:14, RSV).

One who would have a friend must be willing to be a friend, and that includes letting down your ecclesiastical hair and theological defenses! (See Prov. 18:24.) One who would be a friend must recognize that he cannot be friends with everyone, but only can best be a friend with the ones who nurtures and calls forth his best self. An immature, flighty, indifferent, uncompassionate person might be attracted to the minister and his family, but such a personality would not possess the traits to be an authentic friend. One who would be a friend must be willing both to listen and to speak to his friend. A minister has so many occasions to listen to others express their feelings. He needs to cultivate the ability to relate his own feelings. However, he must not short-circuit the friendship by allowing his friend no time to speak. Such a one-way relationship would be nothing more than counselee-counselor, not friend-friend.

One minister groups his friends into three categories: the pastoral group, the hobby group, and the grace group.[2] The pastoral group includes those friendships cultivated among his colleagues in the ministry. People who shared similar hobby interests with him were those who comprised the "hobby group" of friends. The "grace group" were those "people who surfaced from nowhere and offered gifts of love." [3]

God knows the need of friendships for the parsonage dwellers! He will help to provide the gift of caring persons when the minister and his family are open, responsive, and receptive to the gifts of people God sends them. Often the dearest friend may come at the most unlikely occasion or in the most unsuspected person. Beyond loneliness and multiple social contacts, there can be friends!

Two facts are important to remember in any discussion of friendship. First, it is imperative to remember that your family members can be among your best friends! The minister's family should not forsake one another's needs. God has given you to each other to love and enjoy! In the second place, remember that God is your truest, most faithful friend. His everlasting arms are always ready to receive you!

> What a fellowship, what a joy divine,
> Leaning on the everlasting arms

How blessed are you, twice blessed are you, when the everlasting arms of Christ are opened to you in the life of a true friend!

---

[1] Kenneth E. Hayes, Project Analyst, "The Critical Personal Needs of Pastors," June 1976, p. 32; "Pastors' Wives Survey," July, 1976, p. 28.

[2] Dan Kenneth Phillips, "Combating Ministerial Loneliness," *Church Administration,* November, 1977 p. 28.

[3] *Ibid.*

10

Dealing with Fatigue

A discussion one day in an associational ordination advisory council revealed an interesting insight. Not a single man had upon his ordination been given any guidance or suggestions for developing and maintaining physical and spiritual strength. During the course of interviewing numerous candidates for ordination during that year, it was discovered that not a single man had a regular, systematic plan for gaining physical energy. Most men had some approach for acquiring spiritual growth, but not one—ranging in age from a college student to a man in his forties—was in the best physical condition.

Evidently the practical and theoretical models for ministers have been placing all the emphasis on performing and accomplishing, with little attention devoted to developing the strength necessary for the work. The work of the minister is very demanding on him physically and emotionally. Unless he is preparing himself during the calm to withstand the storm, he will easily be swept under by the forces of the multiple physical and emotional stresses.

Many hours are spent in study and preparation for worship, meetings, and counseling. Coupled with the worship tasks, usually three times a week for several denominations (Sunday morning, Sunday night, and Wednesday night, though some men preach twice on Sunday morning), are the numerous other demanding, draining responsibilities of the minister.

A man who once served one of the largest churches of the nation confided that one of the biggest obstacles in his work was discovering, training, and maintaining a competent staff. A large number of churches do not have multiple staff members, but every church has either a staff to administer or lay church leaders to organize, train, and administer. The planning, organizing, personal discussion with the leader, and the sheer hours involved in meetings themselves can drain the energy of the strongest minister. The nature of their personality and approach to ministry enable some ministers to thrive on administrative work, but even with them strength is being sapped.

The majority of ministers carry some teaching responsibility, be it on Sunday morning, Sunday night, Wednesday night, a special group during the week, or a class taught at a nearby college or seminary. Preparation time as well as the lecture itself demand energy from the minister.

The community places a burden on the strength of many ministers. Helping agencies expect ministers to serve on the boards. In the South almost every community event desires to have the respectability and blessing of a "clerical" prayer—all the way from horse shows to Easter egg hunts from safety patrol trips, to ball games, from a neighboring church's lectureship, to the dedication of a new industry. Physical and emotional energy are consumed in both attending the event and in attempting to offer an honest, authentic prayer in that environment.

A weak man could not stand up under the strain of sixteen to eighteen hour workdays, with the added load of answering telephone calls from troubled people during the middle of the night or going to be with a family that has just experienced the death of a loved one. Being on call twenty-four hours a day, seven days a week, builds up a tremendous stress level in the life of both the minister and his family. Overshadowing the whole experience is the burden of living with the role expectations of the minister—some that are self-imposed, some that are learned from ministerial models, and some that are directed by the congregation. It becomes difficult to relax as long as one is still near the mountains of work and the multitudes of people that need the minister's attention. And thus the push, push, push continues and the stress builds higher and higher.

When a man is weary physically and/or emotionally, he is most susceptible to making mistakes, upsetting someone, or becoming passionately upset himself. Most often the minister's feelings about the problems within the congregation or the problems between the people and him are dumped on his wife. He asks, "Who will be my shepherd, my minister?" She asks, "Where will I dump all the garbage he puts in my lap?" Most men confide more freely and fully in their wives than any other person. But where does he go for help? And how can she avoid having to bear the brunt of his hurt and stress?

People in the helping professions have been termed "hidden victims" when people are involved in crises. In other words, the doctors, nurses, reporters, ministers, and funeral-home people are some of those who are indirectly involved in the pain and grief of others, and they must have some way to express their feelings. Most often the more professional a person is, the greater the temptation to hide his feelings behind his work. Instead of being able to cry or to be silent with one who is grieving, instead of saying there is no pat answer or easy way out, a minister is often guilty of succumbing to the professional temptation to turn off his feelings by trying to offer blanket consolation to those who are hurting.

The end result of this behavior is that the minister has to do something with his feelings. He can either go to the source of his feelings and deal directly with them, or he will choose some other outlet—perhaps an inappropriate one—to ventilate his feelings. The remaining option is to play perpetually defensive games and hide feelings until one has a nervous breakdown, a physical disorder, a marital blowup, or a vocational disaster. Feelings can be stuffed in the corner of one's life just so long, and then eventually they must come to the surface in some way, shape, or fashion.

There are numerous advantages in developing and maintaining some means of strengthening oneself physically. For one thing, physical exercise is an essential complement to the intense intellectual and emotional work a minister performs. While a man may have difficulty in "leaving his work at the office," when he gets busy with one of his forms of physical activity, his mind can be freed and his body relaxed.

Physical exercise is also important to keep the body strong and useful. Ministers preach Paul's admonition that "the body is the temple of the Holy Spirit" (1 Cor. 6:19), but they usually are referring to nothing more than staying away from alcohol, drugs, tobacco, and illicit sex! The truth is every overweight minister is a walking denial of the meaning of this verse! We are to care for this habitation God has given us, not just for our comfort, but also in order that our ministry may be long, unhindered by unnecessary illness or disability due to poor physical habits.

Physical activity and relaxation are also helpful in that a minister has something to do when he retires. For the time of illness, disability, and/or retirement, every minister should have some type of indoor physical activity or hobby. This may take the form of furniture refinishing, furniture building, macrame, latch rug hooking, model building, electronic work, stamp collecting, coin collecting, or any number of other interesting hobbies. A few minutes devoted to one's hobby each day can help relax some of the accumulated tension.

Similarly, every minister would greatly benefit by having some regular outside physical activity. In recent years a great deal has been written about the value of jogging. After a doctor's examination and approval, a gradually developed plan of walking and jogging can be very therapeutic for a minister of any age. Twenty to thirty minutes of vigorous exercise at least three or four days a week will improve both the respiratory and circulatory systems of the body. When the lungs are kept at peak efficiency and the blood vessels do not get clogged, the heart has a much easier job. Further, regular running will lower the pulse rate by 10 to 20 beats a minute, providing additional relief for the heart. Consistent running of a few hours a week will help tone muscles and trim fat.

The benefits of running do not cease with the enumeration of the physical advantages. Running also has some very real psychological pluses. Part of this is due to how much concentration is needed to discipline yourself to run. After laying aside all the excuses not to run and then getting out to run, a person will discover that his mind will be freed of all else. After the first 15 to 20 minutes, the average runner feels a real sense of exhilaration and peace. The rhythm of running, the fresh air, and the sense of accomplishment all figure into this psychological boost. Also, doctors have observed that running gets more oxygen into the bloodstream and thereby increases the capacity of the brain. A runner feels better and thinks more clearly. And due to the satisfaction of oxygen in the blood, his system craves less food, which is another, but potentially fattening, means of trying to satisfy the energy level. Jogging can be a family activity as well as a solo exercise.

Running is not the only outside exercise a minister and his family might develop. Tennis, swimming, biking, soccer, and vigorous walks are examples of other sports that offer good, fast exercise. A great many people find thorough relaxation in golfing, though the average course today allows for little walking due to the rush for the players to ride through.

Another means of dealing with physical and emotional stress is to attempt to increase stress and then relax it. A person can focus on only one thing at a time, so when one's body and mind are really tense, a good exercise is to try holding your arm out just as rigid as you can for 30 to 60 seconds. Then slowly release it and let it drop to your side, concentrating on the feeling of total relaxation as your arm is loosened. After doing this exercise with both arms two or three times, you will have been able to get a handle on your stress by increasing it and then being in control of releasing it.

Using the concentration power of your mind can provide a means of stress release. Through practice and discipline you can come to the point of being able to think on nothing other than a pleasant experience or the most beautiful scene you can project in your fantasy. After spending 5 to 10 minutes enjoying those delightful feelings, your previous tension will be greatly decreased.

Surely one of the best means of dealing with physical and emotional stress is to be aware of the source of stress and deal directly with it. The suggestions of the last several paragraphs have been means of coping with the results of stress, but the cause is still present until a person recognizes it and comes to grips with it.

For example, many ministers feel they are in the only profession that goes through a midlife crisis. After all, it is a fact that after a man reaches forty or forty-five, some churches begin to shy away from him because they want a "younger" man who will appeal to the youth and young adults. The fact is, psychologists are now writing that *every* adult goes through continuing stages, crises, passages, and chapters, of life. And it is during the long thirty-five to fifty-five year era when one moves into middle age that the feelings of failure, of not reaching the goals set in younger years, or of being a disappointment to oneself and his family creep into the minds of many adults! Knowing that midlife changes are normal and natural aids in one's adjustment and ability to cope.

Quite a bit has been mentioned earlier about having time alone for communion with God. There is no way to overemphasize the importance of developing and maintain spiritual discipline as a means of becoming all God intends a person to be; as a means of developing wholeness; as a means of enjoying doing one's job well; as a means of developing a loving family; as a means of coping with stress.

Bruce Grubbs reported that in a Southern Baptist Convention Sunday School Board project on stress within ministers that as stress increases the devotional life decreases. Ministers become just like Elijah when he felt he was the only one in the land who was worshiping God. And, just like Elijah, the minister is most susceptible to such a low immediately following a high experience such as Elijah's victory over the priests of Baal. Read through 1 Kings 19 to receive a picture of how Elijah coped with his stress. At times his coping was positive but at other points he failed to deal creatively with stress.

Spiritual discipline never has and never will come easily. It requires time, planning, creativity, variety, and consistency to maintain devotional reading, thoughtful reading of the Word, prayer, and meditative listening to God. Of course, any discipline is difficult and costly. But the results of spiritual discipline are power and freedom from the feelings of estrangement from God and his purpose.

The tendency is for the devotional life to wane when one becomes discouraged under physical and emotional stress. Beware that under the very same circumstances the minister's morals may also let down their barriers. When a man begins to feel sorry for himself, he can justify some types of wrong he normally would stand strong against. For example, a man may begin to slack off on his work and not do a fair day's work for a fair day's pay. Or other men may become entangled in theft, embezzlement, or adultery—all in the midst of feeling depressed from stress and seeking some means of being uplifted. Jesus' admonition remains crucial for the minister and his family today: "Come to me, all who labor and are heavyladen, and I will give you rest. Take my yoke upon you, and learn from me; for I am gentle and lowly in heart, and you will find rest for your souls. For my yoke is easy, and my burden is light" (Matt. 11:28-30).

No one is able to deal with a crisis with any more strength than that which he brings to the crisis. Therefore it is crucial that a minister be able to get in touch with his own feelings as well as be able to express his feelings to someone else. It may be a ministerial friend or professional colleague with whom a minister can share the fallout of being a "hidden victim." Or it may be that when a congregation realizes that their minister is human, that he reveals he, too, has feelings, that they will be able to offer a greater supportive ministry to him physically and emotionally.

What are some indications that a man is positively coping with physical and emotional stress? If a man is able to identify, own, and be responsible for his feelings, he is coping with stress. If a man is able to be in touch with God and be sensitive and responsive to his presence and direction, he is coping with stress. If a man is able to touch others— to understand their feelings and express Christian warmth and compassion through a smile, a handclasp, or an arm around the shoulder—he is coping with stress. If a man has devised a personal scheme of exercise and relaxation, he is coping with stress. If a man can help others bear their burdens without coming apart at his own seams, he is coping with stress. If a man can admit the tensions and strains of his own life and seek the guidance of God, he is coping with stress. Then he is able to proclaim with the psalmist the meaningful words of contentment:

> O Lord, my heart is not lifted up,
>   my eyes are not raised too high;
> I do not occupy myself with things
>   too great and too marvelous for me.
> But I have calmed and quieted my soul,
>   like a child quieted at its mother's breast;
>   like a child that is quieted is my soul (Ps. 131:1-2).

11

Neglecting Not the Family

Half a century ago most of America's families lived in the country or in small towns. The entire family was a rather close-knit group working with the father in whatever his occupation might have been. Dialogue among family members took place on the job and regularly at mealtime. Children learned from their parents by watching them and working with them. The members of the family seldom did anything apart from the family unit.

For the most part all of that is now a day gone by. With few exceptions children are not around their parents enough to learn from them concerning their work. The minister's family could be such a wonderful exception, though truthfully ministerial family life is not always recognized in such a valued light. Though the family does get to observe the minister in one of his primary functions as worship leader/proclaimer, they still feel as separate from him as do the families of so many other professionals.

There are some stresses that are common to all families, such as the need for regular, in-depth, meaningful interaction between husband and wife and parents and children. Also, there is the common need for private time for each individual as well as the need for the family to be with their extended or surrogate family. Every other stress described in the life of the minister culminates in the description of the stress of the family. Education, mobility, church, economics, time, social, physical, emotional, and all other stresses funnel into the boiling pot of tension that contributes to the life of the minister's family. These multiple stresses tend to create and compound stress in the lives both of the individual family members and the entire family unit.

A minister must stop and take inventory to determine his priorities. Unless he feels that his love for God is followed by his love for his family, he may be dragging his family down the drain emotionally if not spiritually. Some ministers may try to claim that a man of God must put God's work before his family. This notion is blasphemous according to the Word of God! William Barclay translated the crucial text from 1 Timothy this way: "A man who had not succeeded in making a Christian home could hardly be expected to succeed in making a Christian Church. A man who had not instructed his own household and family could hardly be the right man to instruct the family of the Church. Church work is no virtue and no credit to a man, if in the performance of it, he neglects his own home and family. Like charity, Christian work begins at home" [1] (1 Tim. 3:4-5, Barclay).

The family stands a chance with the stress under which it lives only if and when the minister begins to offer them some of his quality time and attention instead of the leftovers. The family might survive the ordeal the minister lives with when he honestly wants them and resolutely commits himself to them.

Children are perceptive to how their parents feel about them. The time their parents spend with them, the way they are looked at, the manner in which their parents talk to them cause them to know early in life whether or not they are truly loved and cared for—in spite of what their minister/father might say about Christian love from the pulpit! Children are not interested in the theory of Christian love. They want to see and experience it for themselves! One night a little boy told his parents good night and within a short time asked for someone to come tuck him in. When he was told he had been tucked in, he asked for a drink of water. Upon hearing he had already consumed two glasses of water, he asked for someone to come sleep with him, because he was afraid of the dark. In desperation his mother said he should not be afraid because God was with him. He called back, "I know . . . but I want somebody with SKIN on 'em!" [2] And so it is—children want concepts that are warm, genuine, and personal which they can experience with their parents.

Whether or not the minister realizes it, his children often tend to reject his interests, standards and values—whether directly or by rebelling in opposition to him. Instead of using power and cold reasoning to deal with the problems and needs of children, the message of love of Jesus Christ compels parents to use honesty, humility, understanding, reasonable expectations, clear family rules, compassionate listening, and consistent follow-through for improper behavior.

Any parent, including a pious minister, can browbeat his child into submissive obedience for a few years, but sooner or later, unless he has built a warm human relationship, he will lose all significant ties with that child.

Once a little boy came into the house with his bat and ball, complaining to his father that he asked the coach to let him play, but the coach never seems to listen to him. With a troubled look he asked his father why coaches never listen to kids. Then he looked at his father who had continued to read his newspaper, and when he asked him again, his father's only response was "Huh?" No minister can tell his children they are important from the pulpit and then ignore them in the parsonage. No minister can expect his children to develop Christian graces unless he is practicing them in his home.

Parenting is the most important profession in the world, and yet, most of us are so ill-prepared for this responsibility and treat it so casually. We act as if having the physical ability to reproduce makes us competent to know all about caring for our offspring. The minister who feels his children get in the way of his work should remember that Jesus rebuked his disciples when they tried to keep the little children from coming close to him and taking up his time. Jesus not only took time for the children, placed them on his knee, and talked to them, but he dropped the bombshell by saying that their openness and ready trust characterized the kind of commitment essential for one to become a genuine disciple! (Luke 18:15-17).

Children *daily* need encouragement when low, love when questioning their self-worth, consolation when hurt, forgiveness when mistaken, incentive to live their lives, and nurture to fulfill their potential. Yet all that many children receive— even or especially in the parsonage—is the admonition to do their work and stay out of trouble. The parsonage children, just like all other children, are frequently fed a steady diet of the electronic "drug"—television—as a substitute for time and attention from their father. Many families, many spouses, many parents, and children have lost the ability to talk to one another because the majority of time they are in the house together, someone is listening to one or more televisions. The problem is not only *what* they see but also how many, many hours are spent in viewing— time that might have been spent in helpful dialogue, crucial listening, delightful sharing, or joyful teaching.

Unless a minister is out of town overnight—and the number of nights a year should be carefully guarded for the family's sake—there should be some time gleaned from each day when the entire family can be and share together. For some families this time may be around the supper table or even around the breakfast table. Some ministers might rise to say this would be impossible to schedule. An exchange student from Rhodesia related not only does her family share breakfast, but also they rise to have private and family worship for one hour before breakfast! Instead of watching television every night during the supper hour, the family might take turns with an improvised "show and tell" for the day. Or some families might want to be more thoughtful in their advance planning and have family games around the table.

Whether or not the average minister realizes it, he often abdicates his role of parenting and leaves the bulk of the child-rearing to his wife. This is unfair both to his wife and to his children. The minister may well defend his wife before the church, saying that she will not be considered an unpaid secretary, musician, education or youth worker. But, at the same time, he turns right around and expects her to be an unpaid housekeeper, cook, tutor, purchasing agent, referee, bookkeeper, entertainer, laundress, "home secretary," research assistant, ghost writer, and multipled other tasks. Any woman who feels called of God to live in a parsonage and work alongside her husband will cherish the contributions she can make to Christ's ministry in the Christian church. However, the fact remains it is both a discredit to the minister and a gross injustice to his wife when the bulk of the family responsibilities are hers alone. The two-becoming-one concept in Genesis very definitely includes the childrearing task! Children need both a father and a mother to look to and follow. And whatever parents implant in the hearts and lives of children will very likely be there for a lifetime!

A wife who feels she is on the bottom rung on her husband's list of priorities is likely to withdraw from participation in her "competing lover"—the church. Or she might try to manipulate help from her husband, such as running errands or helping around the house. If she fails to receive genuine love, support, or understanding, she will settle for a divorce rather than continue an indefinite relationship under her present circumstances. Children who feel they are always left out of their father's main plans may abandon their father as soon as possible—leaving home literally and dropping the moral and religious teaching he propounded so eloquently. Likewise, a church that observes a minister's ineffectiveness in his own home will not pay close attention to his plea for them to do in their homes what seems to be beyond the grasp of "the man of God." All families live under some forms of stress, and if the minister cannot maintain a sense of balance between personal, professional, and family claims on him, he can bring to bear little influence on those among whom he ministers. It is possible for ministers both to strengthen their families and to model positive family living by publicly announcing a designated night of the week as "family night" in the parsonage—a night that will not be usurped except by rare life or death emergencies. While some ministers have been working so hard to prove their worth to their congregation or to God, they have neglected their responsibilities nearest them—their families. The gospel of grace preached on Sunday should be daily taught and enacted at home.

A couple who had been married over fifty years advised couples who would emulate them to tell each other more often how much they love each other. Ministers who talk so much in the church buildings and public places often lose their tongues in their own home with their wife and children. Similarly, the ministers who advocate honesty and openness in relationships frequently live out stereotyped roles in their home or play manipulative games with their family. A caring man of God will seek to cope with the stresses within his family instead of seeking an easy way out. Several years ago Seward Hiltner reported in his insightful book, *Ferment in the Ministry,* that one denomination offered ministers and families a one-week or two-week psychiatric evaluation relatively cost free. This service was done in complete privacy with no report made to the denomination. A follow-up evaluation of this service disclosed an amazing fact. "Ministers appeared who, after investigation, proved to be no more mentally ill than other people, but who really hoped that the psychiatrists could call them such—because then the relational problems in the church, or in the family, would not have to be taken as their own responsibility. One could almost say that unconsciously they wanted to be regarded as 'sick.' " [3] What could be a more convenient cop-out than to be able to say "I'm sick," and thus eliminate any responsibility for actions, attitudes, or failures? Of course such an outlook only brings further injury to the minister's family.

A minister who cares about the God he claims to serve will seek to care more genuinely about his family. He will not use overpowering dominance, harsh authoritarianism, or pious guilt-raising techniques to bring his family into submission in order to protect his reputation. Instead, he will seek to express total respect, growing love, and deep affection out of the basic gift of grace and love from God for him. Ultimately the only way the stresses of the family can be met are when the minister sees his loved ones as gifts of God and treats them as such.

Real family sharing which is genuine and consistent is a real key to coping with stress in the parsonage. It is exciting that what is learned, taught, and preached can become a living reality within the parsonage and the influence of its inhabitants. Sharing vital concerns, engaging in family worship, caring for people in need, praying for one another, forgiving mistakes, demonstrating patience, allowing space to be individuals, calling forth one another's gifts, discussing the Bible studied, and having time for each other are but a few of the ways that the minister, his wife, and their children can implement in their life-style the concepts they publicly espouse and have personally internalized.

This is not to say that the minister or his family ever fully arrives in the matter of grasping all the dimensions of Christian living. But the exciting potential of this unique family is they have the awareness and the tools to accomplish so much together in the name of Christ. The family that sees themselves as workers together for God's purposes has taken an important step in coping with the stress that comes into the minister's family.

Effective family life is a pressing need in our society today. If the minister and his family can take seriously the importance of meaningful family life, they can accept the possibility of being a witness to the world of how Christ can transform existence into living.

The most hardened pagan will sit up and take notice of a family which has learned to live well together—a family where husband and wife show mutual love and respect, and the children are polite and well-behaved. Those who have not found a good family life nevertheless want to. Those who do not have satisfying relationships in their own homes nevertheless look with favor on those who do. Those who have not raised up their children well nevertheless admire those who have. Those who families are barren of love and laughter and friendly interchange nevertheless look with undisguised envy at the family up the street which has such a good time together.[4]

The admonition of Paul gives the minister's family its greatest tool for coping with its stresses: "Christ's message in all its richness must live in your hearts. Teach and instruct one another with all wisdom. Sing psalms, hymns, and sacred songs; sing to God with thanksgiving in your hearts. Everything you do or say, then, should be done in the name of the Lord Jesus, as you give thanks through him to God the Father" (Col. 3:16-17, TEV).

So may it be!

[1] William Barclay, "The Daily Bible Study," *The Letters to Timothy, Titus and Philemon* (Philadelphia: The Westminster Press, 1960), pp. 85-86.

[2] Jack Elrod, "Winky Ryatt," *The Charlotte Observer,* May 14, 1978.

[3] Seward Hiltner, *Ferment in the Ministry* (New York: Abingdon Press, 1969), p. 19.

[4] Larry Christenson, *The Christian Family* (Minneapolis: Bethany Fellowship, Inc., 1974), p. 199.

PART 3

Introduction

One has said, "Stress follows us through life like a shadow and it does not disappear merely because we look away from it. . . . Stress goes with purposeful activity the way mist rises from a swiftly running river or clouds of dust swirl above an army marching across the desert. It is stressful to be alive, to love, to be disappointed, to meet deadlines, and to do any of the countless other things that make up the substance of our inhabiting the human situation." [1]

Therefore, since stress is a normal part of living, for ministers' families the real question becomes: "How can we, in the name of Christ, cope with stress in a redemptive and creative way?" The emphasis of the last section of this book focuses upon a challenge for ministers' families to consider as part of their Christian witness their efforts at coping with stress. The congregation that observes *one* Christian family dealing with the stress of living in a powerful and productive way has a good model for themselves. The key to making this witnessing opportunity a workable one is for Christ to be the center of life and to be the "power transformer" that converts incapacitating stresses into storehouses of energy and wholeness. It is only the power of Christ that can bring meaning into disarrayed lives. Only Christ can bring peace and calmness to anxious, struggling people.

---

[1] Eugene Kennedy, *Living with Everyday Problems* (Chicago: Thomas More Press, 1974), p. 79.

12

Guidelines for Coping with Stress

One day Linus walked up to Lucy and told her that he had just seen a dog in the back of a station wagon parked near the grocery store. The windows were slightly down and the dog was barking and barking. He wondered why he was barking—if he were hot, afraid, mad, or lonely. Then Linus saw Snoopy lying on the top of his doghouse and he said to Lucy that if only Snoopy could talk, perhaps he could tell them why the dog was barking. Snoopy sat up, watched the two walk away, and said to himself, "I wouldn't even try. There are some things you can never explain to a layman." [1] And so it is! It seems there are some aspects of the life and stress of a minister and his family that lay people cannot fully understand. However, one need not throw up his hands in frustrated self-pity and lonely despair. Though not all will understand the special aspects involved in being the minister's family, there is One whose understanding is all-encompassing and never ending. He is the rock and shelter in a weary land and brings refreshment and nourishment to those who allow him.

All of us must recognize that stress is an unavoidable dimension of life, but we do have a choice in regard to it! "We can become the masters of stress or we must become its victims." [2] In their book, *Thrive on Stress,* Robert Sharpe and David Lewis propose the theory that "properly controlled and used, stress can be the best thing that ever happens to you. Once you have learned the procedures which enable you to master stress you will find that it is no threat to your survival and success but a powerful creative force which can transform your life for the better . . . . Stress can harm you when it runs riot in your life. Learn to control and use it and you will be able to live a healthier, happier, more successful and more fulfilled life." [3]

These authors recognize the damaging and dangerous aspects of uncontrolled stress. At the same time, their insights give us the challenge that we can harness stress for creative purposes. We who are Christians and have the power and strength of Christ within us can even more readily affirm the positive aspects of stress and use it to help us reach greater heights for him.

In the preceding eight chapters we have given some suggestions for coping with specific stresses. Overarching these suggestions there are some general guidelines which can serve to help the ministers' families creatively respond to the inevitable stresses of their lives.

Properly focus your priorities and be ready to evaluate and readjust them regularly.

> Flexibility and adaptability, which allow for emergencies and even "plan for the unexpected," can be a real boost in coping with the stress of planning family and personal time.

Develop mutual family interests, as well as individual interests.

> Biking, walking, jogging, rock collecting, stamp collecting, reading classics together can offer not only family leisuretime outlets but also contribute to physical and intellectual growth.

Learn how and when to get away from the stresses.

Mini-retreats of ten minutes during the day, an hour apart, a day away, or a series of days can lighten a heavy mind and heart and renew a sagging spirit.

Love one another with honesty, compassion, and fullness.

Nothing aids in overcoming stress and emotional fatigue as much as the knowledge that one is loved regardless of all other circumstances; love is indeed a haven of rest.

Enjoy being a family and enjoy being the minister's family.

Have fun with each other and affirm the worth of each person as a unique gift of God.

Learn to appreciate experiences of "serendipity"—those spur-of-the-moment times of pleasure and happiness which happen to open hearts.

Unexpected opportunities to relax, to meet a friend, to visit a special place, to sit and share one's inner feelings require little effort and time but return great benefits.

Remember who you are and whose you are.

Recognizing one's abilities, feelings, dreams, and hopes in light of one's calling from God assists in shedding proper light on times of stress and assures one he is not alone in his efforts.

"Bloom where you are planted."

Be content and willing to blossom in the circumstances of your present life and waste not precious days in longing and self-pity.

Avoid unreasonable competition with yourself, your peers, your family.

> Know your own self, affirm your strengths, and commit your weaknesses into the transforming hands of God.

Keep on trusting in the power and goodness of God.

> Let your knowledge of the wisdom of God be the stack pole around which you tie all of the experiences and meaning of your life.

Stress, in our society, is inevitable. It is part of the fabric of life. But we have a stronghold who is Jesus Christ. He has been where we are. He knows our distresses, our fears, our anxieties, and our hurts. It is to him we go as teacher and encourager. In times of weariness and confusion, look to the cross of Christ which reminds us of the lengths to which God has gone to provide help and hope for us.

> I take, O Cross, thy shadow
>   For my abiding place;
> I ask no other sunshine than
>   The sunshine of his face;
> Content to let the world go by,
>   To know no gain or loss,
> My sinful self my only shame,
>   My glory all the cross.[4]

It takes work, effort, faith, Bible study, and prayer to deal with stress. Through it all Christ is the key! We cannot face and endure stress alone and emerge victorious. We cannot ignore and deny stress and come away in one piece. We cannot pour out the frustration of our stress on our church and maintain a semblance of the redeeming body Christ intended his church to be. But, we can, in the power and might of Christ, learn to discover the strength and ability to cope with our stress.

A vital factor to bear in mind is that we are doing the work of Christ in his name! Any minister who wishes to be happy and effective must come to grips with the fact he is a servant "who works at somebody else's convenience." [5] A minister must take care not to seek parity with other so-called "service professions," a great many of which do not deserve the name because they are not servants! If you feel they are servants, try to reach a garage's service department or a social service office on a holiday weekend!

It is possible to be professionally trained and earn a living by repairing broken bodies, broken cars, and broken homes and still not be related to the servant Jesus described in his parable. (See Luke 17:7-10.) It is not possible to be a faithful minister of the gospel, to be professionally trained and earn a living by repairing broken souls, without being related to the servant whom Jesus described in the parable. A pastor serves people precisely at their convenience. He works while they rest and waits on tables while they eat, or else he comes into conflict with them and into conflict with himself.[6]

Furthermore, a servant does not expect to be thanked for his work. "People didn't thank Jesus because he went about doing good. A few were grateful for him, but society as a whole put him on a cross. The world often gives that treatment to those who serve it." [7]

A minister and his family who are aware of who they are and in relation to each other are on the way to victorious living with Christ. They know the risks and the cost, but travel on bravely because the Savior has already traveled the road and paved the course.

It is God who has called you to a special life, a unique ministry. It is he "who has called you out of darkness into his marvelous light. Once you were no people but now you are God's people; once you had not received mercy but now you have received mercy" (1 Pet. 2:9-10). Put away your dark masks and sing a song of gladness because God has called you to be special people for him! Go then—and be those people!

[1] Charles Schultz, "Peanuts," *The Charlotte Observer,* August 20, 1978.

[2] Robert Sharpe and David Lewis, *Thrive on Stress* (New York: Warner Books, 1977), p. 19.

[3] *Ibid.,* p. 18.

[4] Elizabeth C. Clephane, "Beneath the Cross of Jesus."

[5] Leonard Griffith, *We Have This Ministry* (Waco: Word Books, 1973), p. 55.

[6] *Ibid.*

[7] *Ibid.,* p. 57.

Epilogue

Robert Raines, in his book, *To Kiss the Joy,* asserts that in the final analysis the clue to life is to "trust the process" and "flow with the river."

If we think of our lives like the flow of a river, we realize there is a timing, a tide in our being and in our relationships . . . . When we come really to believe deep down that the flow of our lives, the underlying currents that are moving in us and about us, are not against us but are for us, that the Spirit of God is literally in the flux and movement of our lives, then it becomes possible for us to go with the flow of our lives in the confidence that God is with us literally in everything.[1]

Hallelujah, God is with each of us in all things! He makes it possible for us to cope with stress and to live creatively in his world.

---

[1] Robert A. Raines, *To Kiss the Joy* (Waco: Word Books, 1973), pp. 141-42.

SCRIPTURE REFERENCE INDEX